THE *Bride* MADE READY

Instructions to Prepare the Hearts of God's People

Judith Lyon Kesselman

Carpenter's Son Publishing

www.touchofheaven.org

info@touchofheaven.org

The Bride Made Ready: Instructions to Prepare the Hearts of God's People

Published by Carpenter's Son Publishing, Franklin, Tennessee

Published in association with Larry Carpenter of Christian Book Services, LLC
www.christianbookservices.com

Cover Illustration by Charles Piccirilli

Cover and Interior Design by Suzanne Lawing

Edited by Andrew Toy

Printed in the United States of America

978-1-940262-99-4

CHAPTER 1

THE MARRIAGE IS ON

For the eyes of the LORD run to and fro throughout the whole earth, to shew himself strong in the behalf of them whose heart *is* perfect toward him. (2 Chron. 16:9a)

We live in a crucial moment of eternity. The bride of Christ is summoned to arise in radiant beauty to dispel darkness and prevail in God's strength over all manner of evil on the earth. Thereby we honor and glorify our beloved Lord and King. This is the church's closing season for maturation and holy transformation. We are on the edge of the final global dissemination of His truth in manifest presence and power through us. The stakes are very high: billions of lost souls dying without Christ. Our Lord's plan for these days in which we now live was carefully hidden away within His Word for those who seek and keep seeking Him. Just as Abraham commissioned his servant Eliezer to procure a suitable bride for his only son Isaac, so God, the Father, has sent forth His Holy Spirit to diligently search "throughout the earth to show Himself strong on behalf of those whose heart is perfect [mature or blameless] toward him" (2 Chron. 16:9). He is searching for believers sincerely devoted and totally set apart for Him and His present-day purpose.

He is seeking those whose love is without restrain and tirelessly pursue true intimacy with Him. He is chasing after those whose passion for Christ directs their action no matter the price.

Eliezer swore that he would not choose a bride from among the daughters of the Canaanites but from within Abraham's kindred or house. Likewise, the Holy Spirit is presently stirring hearts within the household of God—the church. The bride *being made ready* is chosen and called out from among the slumbering church of Christ (Eph. 5:14-16). This is not the sleep of death before Christ but a drowsy walk in Christ. Jesus said, "Many are called but few are chosen. He that hath an ear, let him hear what the Spirit saith unto the churches" (Rev. 3:22). The whole church is saved. The whole church is the bride of Christ, but only those who willfully respond to the calling of the Holy Spirit in this hour will be made ready to display His glory in these last of last days. And so they will reap a vast harvest of souls to fill His house in His tribute before His return. By His Spirit the bride made ready will also arouse the residue of the church still numbly sedated by the world to the same passionate course and expectation.

When Eliezer found Rebecca, one willing to go wherever God's Spirit would lead her, he placed upon her a gold earring and two gold bracelets. These called-out, passionate seekers of God will be beautifully adorned with the fruit of the Holy Spirit as they are molded to live a lifestyle of *agape* love. His divine nature will abound in His bride made ready as she truly abides in Him (John 15:4). Then Christ in her will show Himself strong by demonstrating His power on her behalf, for love never fails (1 Cor. 13:8) and love activates the faith necessary for the miraculous (Gal. 5:6). The gifts of the Spirit (working of miracles, healing the sick, and even raising the dead) will re-emerge as this loving end-day bride willfully follows His leadings and receives the relentless probing and refinement of the Holy Spirit (Mal. 3:2-3). Upon her preparation and transformation, His glory shall shine *in* and *upon* and *through* her (Isaiah 60:1-2), for she fully expresses His character and compassion to a lost and dying world. And it will not be heavy labor for her. She will waltz with ease as a princess in the arms of her prince across the dance floor of the world amid the most magnificent grandeur of revival that creation has ever witnessed on the earth! Are you ready? Do you want to *be made ready*?

By now you are asking, "Is this not intended for all the church as the bride of Christ?" Yes it is, but only those who are willing to be prepared will be ready to participate in this divine engagement *while yet on earth*. In the parable of the ten virgins awaiting the bridegroom, Jesus clearly declared that only those who "were ready" would enter into the marriage. Note that that is *marriage*, not heaven.

> **[A]nd they that were ready went in with him to the marriage: and the door was shut. (MATT. 25:10b)**

This word "marriage" is translated from the Greek word *gamos* meaning "intimate union with Christ."[1] It is not limited to a particular meal or occasion but an enduring and deepening fellowship. All ten virgins represent the Kingdom of God or body of Christ of whom only those full of His Spirit were accounted as wise and ready (Matt. 25:1-10). They were ready to demonstrate and communicate this divine union with Christ while yet here on earth before our rapture and His second coming. The "ready" of *this* verse is the Greek *hetoimos* meaning "ready, prepared to receive one coming."[2] It is not just ready

[1] Joseph H. Thayer, *Thayer's Greek-Lexicon of the New Testament* (Grand Rapids, MI: Baker Book House, 1977), 109.

[2] Thayer, 255.

to *leave* but ready to receive or be made properly receptive for the appearance of such a worthy, holy One. It comes from an old noun *heteos* meaning "fitness, adjusted, prepared, and made ready." Being made fit for our King is wise in His eyes.

This preparation is also confirmed by the revelation of Jesus Christ as recorded by the apostle John in the book of Revelation.

> **And I heard as it were the voice of a great multitude, and as the voice of many waters, and as the voice of mighty thunderings, saying, Alleluia: for the Lord God Omnipotent reigneth. Let us be glad and rejoice, and give honour to him: for the marriage** [gamos] **of the Lamb is come, and his wife** [bride] **hath made herself ready. (REV. 19:6-7)**

The "ready" of Revelation 19:7 is more detailed than the "ready" of the parable of the ten virgins. It is the Greek *hetoimazo*, which is rendered as "preparing the minds of men to give the Messiah a fit reception and secure his blessings."[3] This also concurs with Matthew and Mark's description of the ministry of John the Baptist before our Lord's first coming: "Behold, I send my messenger before thy face [manifest presence], which shall prepare thy way before thee" (Mark 1:2b). As the awakened church is prepared, her passionate pursuit of Christ will not only prepare the way of our Lord's glorious return but she will also arouse those around her, the lukewarm church and the lost (Jew and Gentile), and beckon them to participate. Multitudes of lives, communities, and even nations will be transformed and receptive to the King of kings.

This is intended for all the church, just as God wills that *all*

[3] Ibid.

men be saved (1 Tim. 2:4). Every member of the body of Christ at new birth is made righteous (2 Cor. 5:21). Each one is adopted and bestowed a relationship with God as Father. But where there is relationship, there is intended to be fellowship. The depth of our fellowship is the indicator of our level of spiritual maturity, intimacy, or readiness. The whole body of Christ is in right-standing with God by the finished work of Christ at the cross, but not all believers are pursuing intimate fellowship with Him that they might be prepared to appropriately herald His second coming by their loving lifestyle. And not all are willing to unite with other believers for this cause. But we must.

This is not a future banquet. This is a holy, supernatural union to be displayed throughout the earth before a lost and dying world which will then continue for all eternity in our Lord's honor. Does this mean that nominal believers will miss heaven? No, but they are more vulnerable to the great falling away of which the apostle Paul warned the church (2 Thess. 2:3). And they could miss experiencing the miraculous ministry of Christ *through* us. Our Lord is coming *to* His church for our sanctification so that He may shine His radiant love and power *through* His church (Isaiah 60:1-2) before He comes *for* His church in the rapture and second coming. He will transform His willing bride so that "when he appears, we shall be like Him" (1 John 3:2) which means "resembling in ability" (power), "condition" (well-being), and "nature" (agape, or unconditional love).[4] That is a glorious bride made ready for our Lord's return!

The church must awaken and get ready! How? Has God provided instructions for the church to be prepared for our Lord's coming? You bet He has. They are hidden away *for us* within Exodus chapter 34. They embody the *keeping* of the Sabbath

[4] W. E. Vine, *An Expository Dictionary of New Testament Words* (Nashville, TN: Thomas Nelson Publishers), 672.

and the three feast seasons of Passover, Pentecost and the Feast of Tabernacles, *not* by the letter of the law as do the Jews but *by His Spirit* (2 Cor. 3:6; Col. 2:16). These collective natural feasts are merely "the shadow of the real substance" (Heb. 8:5; 10:1), the spiritual feasts our Lord Jesus desires His bride to enter into while yet here on earth to come to her full maturity. For us to fully understand His directions for our preparation requires that we first carefully review the originating events commemorated by these holy days or feasts and assay their underlying meaning and divine intent *for us* as New Covenant believers. While we peruse the text of Exodus, we will uncover contrasting and even conflicting differences that will also distinguish the *prepared* or *ready ones* from the church asleep. These accounts were purposefully recorded for us that we might learn from Israel's victories and blunders (1 Cor. 10:5-6) and be made ready and awaken those around us who, at present, are not.

Amid the first eighteen chapters of Exodus, Israel witnessed Almighty God's selective protection for them from the judgments He poured out upon Egypt and her many false gods. The grand finale plague was the death of the firstborn. Israel would be spared but *only* if she obediently followed God's directions. Each family would take a blemish-free lamb, sacrifice it on 14 Nisan (the fourteenth day of the first month of the religious Hebrew year), and apply the blood on their doorposts.

> **And ye shall take a bunch of hyssop, and dip it in the blood that is in the bason, and strike the lintel and the two side posts with the blood that is in the bason; and none of you shall go out at the door of his house until the morning. For the LORD will pass through to smite the Egyptians; and when he seeth the blood . . . the LORD will pass over the door, and will not suffer the destroyer to come in unto your houses to smite you. (EXOD. 12:22-23)**

The blood was applied to the top frame (which would eventually drip to the bottom) and both sideboards. This is the sign of the cross—"the bloodstains" of His nailed hands, feet, and crown of thorns. The lamb was then roasted (just as the Lamb of God tasted the fire of hell on our behalf) and eaten with unleavened bread in readiness to depart Egypt. Unleavened bread would be eaten for seven days as their hasty departure afforded them no time to allow any yeast to rise. With God's favor, they spoiled the Egyptians of their silver, gold, and jewels (Exod. 12:35-36). And they departed without one feeble one in their midst (Ps.105:37). None were ill. So on this original Passover, Israel auspiciously left bondage, poverty, and sickness with great jubilation and thanksgiving to Jehovah God. And He commanded Israel to memorialize this great deliverance by keeping a seven-day remembrance feast annually (Exod. 12:14, 17-20). [This feast season is a precisely painted portrait of our Lord's redemptive work by which we were saved. We bring His work "affectionately to remembrance" every time we take communion (1 Cor. 11:24-25, AMP).]

By Exodus chapter 19 Israel arrived at the foot of Mt. Sinai. Verse 2 says, "Israel camped before the mount." The Hebrew word translated "camped" is *chanach*. It is in the singular form rather than the more commonly used plural form, *machanah*. This seemingly insignificant detail reveals to us an incredibly important insight. Israel was one—they were in unity. They were seeking God *together*. **True unity is a vital, appropriate, and endearing attribute of the bride made ready.** It was *in* Israel's unity that Jehovah God verbally proposed marriage, and should Israel accept His spoken betrothal contract (called an *erusin*), it would become a legally binding marriage contract or covenant. From the erusin, a *ketubah* (written marriage contract or covenant) would be scribed. The ketubah would contain the pledges or obligations of husband and wife to one another as proposed and consented upon verbally.[5] Amid the rejoicing of God's newly liberated people, Jehovah presented His verbal proposal of marriage to *all* of Israel through the mouth of His servant Moses.

> **Now therefore, if ye will obey my voice indeed, and keep my covenant, then ye shall be a peculiar treasure unto me above all people: for all the earth is mine: 6 And ye shall be unto me a kingdom of priests, and a holy nation . . . (Exod. 19:5-6)**

Without hesitation they unanimously agreed and gave their pledge of love to Jehovah God.

> **And all the people answered together, and said, All that the LORD hath spoken we will do. And Moses returned the words of the people unto the LORD. (Exod. 19:8)**

Israel, on the wings of God's awesome deliverance from Egypt, readily accepted His marriage proposal. [We, the church, have been given the same proposal. As Christ's bride we are also "a chosen generation, a royal priesthood, a holy nation, a peculiar people . . . to . . . show forth the praises of him who called us out of darkness" (1 Pet. 2:9), and we are also expected to obey our Lord's voice in our marital covenant with Christ (John 14:21-23), the New Covenant or Testament.]

Next in the Exodus narration, Jehovah God told Moses to *sanctify* the people. Sanctification or holiness is extremely important for preparedness, and it comes in two time frames. Holiness is both a *moment of being set apart* and also *a progressive process of being set apart*. In this case, Israel was at the moment of being set apart for her union with a holy God. [Upon faith in Christ, we too experienced that *moment* and were immediately

5 Our modern ketubah is framed and mounted on a wall in our master bedroom.

sanctified in spirit by the blood of Jesus (1 Pet. 1:2).] Then, on the fiftieth day from leaving Egypt, the original Pentecost, Jehovah God was manifestly present upon Mt. Sinai to wed His beloved Israel. Extravagant excitement filled the air!

> **[T]here were thunders and lightnings, and a thick cloud upon the mount, and the voice of the trumpet exceeding loud; so that all the people that *was*[6] in the camp trembled . . . And mount Sinai was altogether on a smoke, because the LORD descended upon it in fire: and the smoke thereof ascended as the smoke of a furnace, and the whole mount quaked greatly. (Exod. 19:16b, 18)**

Another rendition of this spectacular wedding day was written by the Jewish historian Josephus (Josephus 3.5.2). He described the sky as clear and sunny except for a thick cloud that covered the whole camp of Israel. Though there were no natural signs of bad weather anywhere else, strong winds, thundering, lightening, and showers of rain appeared directly over the Israelites. This holy matrimony was a terrifying experience to the carnal mind and flesh. The people were in great fear and trembling.

Moses then brought Israel to the "nether part of the mount" (Exod. 19:17). This "nether" means "underneath." They were covered under the mount like a Jewish *chupah* or wedding canopy. There, they were wed to Jehovah as Isaiah later proclaimed to Israel, "thy Maker is thine husband. The Lord [Jehovah] of hosts is His name" (Isaiah 54:5a). Jehovah then spoke audibly to the *entire* congregation of Israel, His beloved wife in Exodus chapter 20. He recited to her, her obligations within their marriage contract. Jews call it Torah; Christians call it the Ten Commandments. It is vitally important that we understand that

[6] This verb in singular form is another proof of their unity at that time.

Torah actually means teaching and not law! In fact, Torah is better defined as "revelation for the purpose of sanctification" or "the progressive holiness of soul."

At their initial marital ceremony with Jehovah, Israel was set apart as His in that moment, but with continued fellowship and revelations, she would be progressively and increasingly set apart in life and lifestyle. Israel's husband was revealing Himself to His newlywed wife so that she might come to know Him intimately: His morals, His values, His standards, how He thinks, and how He acts. If she continually pondered or meditated on His Person, she would continually be set apart exclusively for Him and increasingly become more and more like Him. He is holy. She is becoming holy. After all, He is hers and she is His.

[Such is also the arrangement of Christ and the church as the apostle Paul wrote.

> **Husbands, love your wives, even as Christ also loved the church, and gave himself for it; That he might sanctify and cleanse it with the washing of water by the word, That he might present it to himself a glorious church, not having spot, or wrinkle, or any such thing; but that it should be holy and without blemish. (Eph. 5:25-27)**

The Greek word translated "Word" here is *rhema,* which is "a supernatural word of knowledge or revelation." Continued revelations of our Lord to us leads us to the progressive sanctification of our souls. We were instantly made holy in spirit at our rebirth, but the sanctification of our soul continues on. We are called to be "holy in all manner of conversation; because it is written, Be ye holy for I am holy" (1 Pet. 1:15-16). The word "conversation" here does not refer to dialogue but to lifestyle. Jesus, like His Father, desires a pure and holy bride in attitude and action, not just age and appearance.]

Regrettably, Israel as a whole did not embrace the soul sanctification process. Because she did not know God well, she did not trust His intents and methods. She chose *not* to draw near to Him but rather succumbed to fear. Israel *saw* the lightening and the smoking. They *heard* thundering and the trumpet. And they removed themselves and stood afar off (Exod. 20:18-21). They permitted their natural five-sense experience to deprive them of their spiritual inheritance of transformation and beautification. Jehovah God only wished to prove them. Reverential fear is a necessary factor to keep anyone from sin. Moses knew that Jehovah's intentions were honorable. His proving them was for their good that they might walk in His power and might, for Yahweh desired His wedded one to walk as a nation in the miraculous and convert entire people groups to Him throughout the earth. But Israel, as a whole, was not willing to be confronted, cleansed, and conformed to His Word. They wanted to be left alone and left to themselves. Israel (like much of the church today) did not want God meddling with their wrong attitudes, wrong motives, sin, cares, and competing desires. Israel had been delivered from Egypt at Passover, but Egypt still lurked *within* their hearts.

These newlywed Israelites and newly born-again Christians both begin their/our walk with God a bit like a caterpillar. We feel fuzzy-good/God loves us, but we are also earthbound and carnal. But should we choose to submit to the chrysalis of His testing, His proving, and His probing, and if we obey Him no matter what the cost or pain, holy transformation will ensue. Oh, it's uncomfortable. Trials and testing certainly hurt, but they also effectively expose hidden sins and wrong motives of our hearts. Agitated wounds ooze and pain is simply painful and often very messy. But in the end, each proven one will emerge like a radiant butterfly equipped to soar in the heavenlies with Him. This describes "the kingdom of priests" and the "holy nation" of which Jehovah's wife Israel (Exod. 19:6) was to become. It is also the intended perfecting of the church.

Both Moses and Jesus were proven. For Moses it was the two forty-day fasts in the fearsome presence of Yahweh on Mt. Sinai. For Jesus it was the forty days in the wilderness in the evil presence of Satan, after which Jesus returned "in the power of the Holy Spirit" (Luke 4:14). Both covenant heads got into the confining, restrictive cocoon and stayed while Jehovah ministered great transforming pressure to prove them that they might minister in apostolic power and might. All of Israel (like the church) had the right to progressively enter into miraculous ministry through sanctification, but only Moses *pursued* it, *sought* it, and *received* it. How was Moses different? As a type of the bride being made ready, he consistently made three excellent choices.

1. Moses spent quality time in God's presence getting to know Yahweh intimately. When Jehovah wooed Moses to come nigh up on the mount, he readily responded. He spent extravagant time with God receiving more Torah, revelation upon revelation, as recorded in Exodus chapters 21-31. This is revelatory intimacy. Tender love was flowing and intimate fellowship was growing. During the forty-day testing (more like a honeymoon to the bride), Moses received the written marriage contract or ketubah on two stone slabs, the tables of testimony. He had a genuine understanding of Jehovah's character and ways. Very few Old Covenant saints *knew* Yahweh as he did. Most saw the Lord as a wrathful, vengeful God only because they didn't spend enough time to really get to know and trust Him. But Moses knew better. While on the Mount, Jehovah revealed Himself to Moses.

> **And the LORD passed by before him, and proclaimed, The LORD, The LORD God, merciful and gracious, longsuffering, and abundant in goodness and truth.**

Keeping mercy for thousands, forgiving iniquity and transgression and sin . . . (Exod. 34:6-7a)

Shortly after this revelation knowledge, Jehovah promised to do marvels, that is, signs, wonders, and miracles with or through *him* (the faithful one, the one in preparation) but not *them* (the unresponsive church of Israel in general).

The greatest revelation Moses received was of the tabernacle, a habitation of God's presence. This is exceptionally significant to Jehovah God, for the tabernacle symbolizes manifested *union* within their marriage. From the beginning, God had marriage on His mind. Genesis opened with the marriage covenant between Adam and Eve. Revelation closes with the marriage banquet of the last Adam—Christ—and His bride. Jesus' first recorded miracle was at the marriage feast at Cana. Marriage represents an arrangement with us that God has longed for from the beginning: that **the two shall become one.**

The ultimate manifestation of this *union* of Christ and believer is exemplified in the original Feast of Tabernacles. Jehovah God dwelt among Israel in resplendent grace and majesty. His presence was exhibited conspicuously in a cloud by day and fire by night. He was not indistinct or obscure. This was a foretaste of the life and ministry of Jesus Christ our Lord almost two thousand years ago and the far, far more ostentatious display of His glorious presence *in* and *through* His bride made ready soon to emerge throughout the earth. The revived church, multitudes of living mobile tabernacles (like Jesus), are destined to show forth His *Sh'khinah* glory and power in unprecedented proportions before the entire world in these last days as we truly become *one* with Him. It is through His *holy* bride, that His glory will *fill* the earth! Like Moses, the bride who has made herself ready is an *intimate, resplendent bride*, one who knows Him through revelatory knowledge as well as the written Word!

2. Moses listened for and to God's voice. He did not turn back from God, as did Israel; instead, he chose to listen. Israel, in general, forsook her first love the moment they turned away from their opportunity to personally *listen to His voice.* Listening is a prime key to any good relationship, especially marriage. But Israel wrongly opted for Moses to listen *for* them. Their ill decision left them vulnerable to enticement by a false lover—the golden calf—and a future as a nation inundated with spiritual adultery. Is the corporate church today any different? Are we listening to Him and His prophets or are we listening to the voice of opportunities, attractive programs, social issues, and carnal concerns? Are we personally listening for His voice to pursue *His* will for our own lives, or are we just satisfied with a weekly patronizing visit to hear a word from one of the five-fold ministry who *is* listening? Moses did not settle to hear second-hand and we must not either. A prophetic word from another should be primarily for confirmation. All of us must strive to personally listen for God's voice, for it is part of our preparation as His glorious bride. Jesus said that His sheep (not lambs) know His voice, and the apostle Paul expounded that we may all prophesy (1 Cor. 14:31). Like Moses, the bride who has made herself ready is a *listening, prophetic bride.*

3. Moses consistently honored the marital pledge to obey God's voice (Exod. 19:5). When God called him to ascend to the Mount, that is, come up to a higher level of intimacy, Moses responded—he *obeyed.* Of course, such was not the case with all of Israel or the entire church today. By Exodus chapters 32-34 the newly wed Israel committed adultery with the golden calf. Moses, still on the Mount, is informed by Israel's enraged divine Husband of her infidelity toward Him. Fortunately for Israel, Moses interceded on her behalf with a boldness and confidence born out of obedience and intimacy with God. As a result, Jehovah chose not to nullify the marriage and annihilate them.

He could have rightfully blown up Mt. Sinai and stoned His adulterous wife to death. But mercy triumphed over judgment that day when He responded with grace to the intercession of the remnant bride, Moses.

God gave favor to this faithful one in preparation who *was* His wife *in deed* and not in word only, and He turned away His wrath from destroying an entire nation of unfaithful ones. Likewise, the bride of Christ who is made ready *w*ill also plead on behalf of the slumbering church, for our Lord loves each and every one. His mature bride shares His heart's affections. Moses descended from the Mount inflamed with anger with Israel. They had betrayed the One whom Moses dearly loved and revered. Moses demonstratively threw down the ketubah of the marriage covenant they had already broken. Judgment and death by sword and plague consumed those defiant in their adultery. But fortunately, most of Israel took the first step back toward God and union with Him. They humbled themselves and repented of their disobedience (Exod. 33:4). Like Moses, the bride of Christ who is being made ready is *ever repentant of sin* and becoming *increasingly more obedient* to His voice.

While Moses was on Mt. Sinai for the second forty days, Scripture reveals contrasting descriptions between the bride being made ready and the slumbering church (see Exodus chapter 33). For example, Jehovah spoke "face to face" with Moses, whereas Israel only heard secondhand because that was all they desired. Moses came "to know His ways," while Israel only knew His acts (Ps. 103:7). Jehovah promised that His presence would go with *him*, Moses, not *them*, Israel. But again, his intercession brought their inclusion. When Moses requested that Jehovah "show him His Glory," Jehovah agreed and let His goodness pass before *him*, not *them*. The passion of the seeking one compels her to pursue a deeper intimacy than do those of the norm. Today there remains a remnant of Israel zealously pursuing Jehovah God and a remnant within the church passionately in love with His Son. She is being made ready to carry His glory in the end-day revival before His return. Are you one of His remnant lovers?

When Moses returned from the Mount the second time, Scripture records three times that the very skin of his *face shone*, or manifested, the glory of God's holy presence. The shine on Moses' face was the result of his external exposure to *Yahweh's* glory. But the glory upon the bride of Christ who has made herself ready in these end-days will far surpass it. In these last days when darkness touts its evil works and boasts of Satan's strong hold in and among the masses of the world, Isaiah 60:1 says, "Arise, shine; for thy light is come, and the glory of the Lord is risen upon thee." The latter shall exceed the former. The glory of the bride of Christ will far exceed that of Moses because our marriage covenant is better. It is internalized. Christ lives in us. Therefore, the manifestation of His presence or glory in us comes *upon* us from *His rising up within us.*

The radiant light and love of Christ's awakened bride will stand out brilliantly against escalating darkness in the earth. So great will be her brightness that darkness will literally flee from before her face. Those fumbling in darkness will flock to the One shining *within* and *through* her. They will be drawn by the explosive signs, wonders, and miracles bursting forth through the bride in global proportions. Why all the excitement? Because our Groom, the Lord Jesus, is passionately in love with His bride. For centuries He has waited to bring us home to the heavenly place which He has prepared for us. That day is approaching. The clock is ticking away. The time span of this age is running out. The marriage supper is very near. Jesus stands ready to carry us home but not secretly or quietly. No, but rather with a bang—amid the grandest showing of His glory through His church. Are you ready? Are you willing to be made ready? It will be the ride of your life!

CHAPTER 2

THE TWO SHALL BE ONE

For this cause shall a man leave his father and mother, and shall be joined unto his wife, and they two shall be one flesh. (EPH. 5:31)

The ultimate intention for Jehovah's marriage with Israel was that **the two shall become one.** Certainly, husbands and wives are not *one* the day they are betrothed or engaged. They have agreed to unite, and after the marriage ceremony, there will be a union of their flesh as their marriage covenant or commitment to one another is physically consummated in love. But this physical act *alone* does not totally exemplify their union. After all, our core being is spirit. We are spirit-beings with souls occupying flesh bodies. The first marital act of sex may explosively *initiate* the union, but it certainly is not the *completion* of that union. It is a *means*, a very wonderful, productive, God-bestowed means, but it is not the end. It is *a beginning* from which the two will hopefully continue to mutually build upon this natural union—a higher union of spirit and soul.

Israel's explosive sight and sound marriage with Jehovah God at Mt. Sinai was spectacular, but it was not the end, nor was our conversion experience, no matter how awesome it may have been. They are wonderful beginnings from which true lasting fellowship must be nurtured and encouraged to grow. A constant progression toward a perfect union was the earnest desire of Jehovah God with all Israel, but only Moses and a faithful few initially experienced it. After Israel's grievous affair with the golden calf, Jehovah graciously welcomed the *repentant* to restart the process toward a holy manifested union with Him. Likewise, if we will choose to follow God's instruction, we *too* will become one (in soul as well as spirit) with our Lord as did Moses. What are His instructions? We are instructed to keep the Sabbath (Exod. 34:21) and the three feast seasons best known as: Passover (Exod. 34:18), Pentecost (Exod. 34:22a), and the Feast of Tabernacles (Exod. 34:22b). But we do *not* keep them as do the Old Testament saints did by the letter of the law. That is being *religious*! As New Covenant priests in Christ, we keep them by the leading of the Holy Spirit, until it is our genuine *lifestyle in Christ* individually and collectively. This is the rightful result of relationship! Though we may often find our occasions of united celebration occurring right on the Lord's feast days.

It was in 1996 that I first noticed the bride of Christ collectively gathering on the feast days. During the week of Passover, we affectionately remembered the death, burial, and resurrection of our Lord Jesus Christ as a local congregation. Yet every time we have communion, we are bringing to remembrance the Lamb of God slain for our salvation. A few weeks later I was amid a twenty-one-day prayer journey throughout Israel. Ten of those days, I joined about one thousand believers in intercession on the Mount of Olives facing the East Gate for three days and then all around the nation. A handful of us celebrated Pentecost at Ruth Ward Heflin's house on Mt. Zion. It was glorious. Later, during the forty-day period of introspection prior to the Feast of Tabernacles, I noticed our pastor preaching heavy, probing sermons. A seminar on praise was scheduled on both days of the Feast of Trumpets that year, and we kept that feast just as it is meant to be kept, with great rejoicing and excessive, expressive, trumpeting praise. The Day of Atonement that year was *truly* a day of affliction. The whole congregation was called by the senior pastor to briefly fast, not eating lunch, and later attend a solemn assembly that Sunday afternoon to lament the fall of a prominent leader within our midst. The atmosphere was saturated with brokenness. Finally, during the Feast of Tabernacles, on Sunday, September 29, 1996, God's glory manifested strongly in our service. We had kept the feasts! Not as do the Jews but as arranged by God's Spirit. It was but a tiny glimpse to entice us to pursue the greatest outpouring of His Spirit, which is coming soon by purposely keeping His feasts together!

As Gentile believers, we are simply engrafted branches and not life-supporting roots. We draw from our Jewish heritage; they do not draw from us (Rom. 11:15-18). So it behooves us to understand these feasts in natural terms, yet keep them by the Spirit. To the natural Jews, the Sabbath, or *Shabbat*, was and still is observed weekly; the new moon, monthly; and the three feast seasons, yearly. [All (Shabbat, new moons, and the feasts) are repeatedly linked to the East Gate, the entrance and exit of God's glory (1 Ch. 23:31; Ezek. 9:3, 10:4, 10:19, 11:1, 45:17-25, 46:1-12).] The Levites and priests were to keep all these at divinely ordained times. They kept *Shabbat* weekly throughout the nation. But for the three primary feast seasons, the Jewish men in biblical times were required to ascend to the city of Jerusalem in order to keep them collectively.

> **Thrice in the year shall all your menchildren appear before the LORD God, the God of Israel. (Exod. 34:23)**

The New Jerusalem to which we are to ascend is a type of the bride of Christ made ready in splendor before the nations.

> **And I John saw the holy city, new Jerusalem, coming down from God out of heaven, prepared as a bride adorned for her husband. (Rev. 21:2)**

We are to ascend to the appropriate bridal lifestyle by keeping the feasts by the Spirit of the Most High God our Lord and King eternal. His ways for us differ from His ways for Israel, but both covenant people are to keep these feasts.

All three feast seasons originated in Moses' day. Within these three seasons there are a total of seven feasts. In a quick review, the original Passover season was Israel's miraculous deliverance and redemption from slavery, death, and Egypt (Exod. 12-13). It started with the Passover meal and continued for seven days as they fled and fed on unleavened bread. Later, it finished with First Fruits, a celebration of the early harvest,[7] once in the Promised Land. The original Sabbath started when God's people began to rest or trust in His provision of manna on the seventh day (see Exodus chapter 16). The original Pentecost occurred fifty days after the original Passover. It was the magnificent wedding at the foot of Mt. Sinai between Jehovah God and Israel (Exod. 19-20). The original third season, the Feast of Tabernacles, was preceded by the Feast of Trumpets—the completion and dedication of the Tabernacle of Moses [a type of the bride made ready (Exod. 40)]—and the day later called the Day of Atonement, when His holy fire rushed out from His glory before all Israel accepting the priests and their sacrifices (Lev. 9:22-24). The original Feast of Tabernacles was the continual manifest presence of God dwelling among them as a cloud by day and a fire by night. It was a grand ignition of the original revival!

In all, the book of Exodus has forty chapters, the number of testing. All of these feasts are also necessary for our complete

[7] Israel annually has two harvest seasons: the early harvest and the greater latter harvest.

separation from our Egypt and for our transformation. Through these feasts, the bride will be tested and proven, sanctified, and progressively set apart exclusively for Christ, her Groom, by overcoming the worldly, Laodicean spirit (Rev. 3:14-22). We are being purged of the world in order to carry His glory to the lost in these end-days. Why? Christ cannot be one with a bride who has a different mindset than His own. He must not be unequally yoked. Certainly He cannot be yoked with the unsaved. They are spiritually separated from God; they are spiritually dead. Life cannot unite or fellowship with death. But neither can Christ be yoked or one with believers whose inclinations or attitudes are misaligned. Our born-again spirit is of Him, but a spirit other than His own sometimes influences our soul. One day, on the way to Jerusalem, James and John asked Jesus if they should call down destructive fire on a Samaritan city that would not receive Him. Jesus said to them, "Ye know not what manner of spirit ye are of" (Luke 9:55). Their heart intent was askew from His. He came to seek and to save. For two to be *one*, or in union, they must share the same heart attitude, purpose, and plan. These feasts prepare us for such. Keeping them is imperative. Though we keep them differently than did the Old Covenant believers, understanding their history is of preliminary importance.

Within Leviticus 23, there are two Hebrew words translated "feast." One, *chag* (used fifty-six times as "feast" or "feasts"), simply means a "festival" or "solemn feast day." The other word, *mowed* (used twenty-two times as "feast" or "feasts"), provides us with some added insight concerning these feasts. "Mowed" is defined as "an appointment, which is a fixed time or season to assemble; an assembly convened for a definite purpose; congregation; an appointed time, the feast of Jehovah." These feasts are appointments set by Jehovah God for Israel (and those engrafted into Israel through the New Covenant) to meet with Him collectively. They are extremely important to God. So much so that they had a tremendous impact on God's creation plans. The seasons of Genesis 1:14 are not summer, fall, winter, and spring; they are *mowed*, the feasts.

> **And God said, Let there be lights in the firmament of the heaven to divide the day from the night; and let them be for signs, and for seasons** [mowed], **and for days, and years: (Gen. 1:14)**

God created the moon as a celestial clock to enable His beloved people to keep these festivals or appointments with Him. The new moon was a monthly new beginning from which they would count to the start of each feast. The moon often represents flesh, so being new—or least—also reminds us that our flesh cannot discern spiritual things such as God's *kairos*[8] timing. Our flesh must be minimal in guiding us. Our leading must be by His Spirit. As we walk in the Spirit, we will not miss one appointment with our Lord, just as no bride who truly loves her groom is going to miss a date.

Collectively, these feast seasons represent three very meaningful revelations. The first two are:

1. **God's redemptive time table for mankind**

and

2. **Our New Testament marriage covenant in terms of ancient Israeli marriages**

These two are linked together. By the Spirit of God, Leviticus refers to the feasts as "holy convocations" meaning "holy rehearsals." Every time Israel kept a feast, she rehearsed a far more significant event in the realm of the Spirit: the passion of Christ and our wedding rehearsals with Him. What bride would miss her wedding rehearsal? What bride would not gain knowledge of proper bridal etiquette? How about you? Only those who make these rehearsals will be ready to flow in His glory!

[8] Kairos is the Greek word for "time" meaning "a divinely appointed time." It differs from the Greek word "chronos," which refers only to "chronological time."

SEVEN FEASTS in THREE SEASONS

FEAST (Hebrew)	ORIGINAL SCRIPTURE	ORIGINAL EVENT	DATE KEPT	SUMMARY OF FEAST
Passover *(Pesah)* STARTS FIRST SEASON	Exodus 12:1-13, 12:21-28	Exodus from Egypt (Liberty) blood to doorposts	FIRST MONTH 14 Nisan[9]	Leviticus 23:5
Unleavened Bread *(Hag HaMatzah or Hol Hamoed)*	Exodus 12:15-20 13:6-10	Ate unleavened bread for all seven days	14-21 Nisan	Leviticus 23:6a
First Fruits *(Bikkurim)*	Exodus 12:16b Later at first early harvest	Celebrate early harvest	21 Nisan seventh day	Leviticus 23:6b-14
Pentecost *(Shavuoth)* SECOND SEASON	Exodus 19-20	Marriage Covenant Jehovah & Israel receive Torah	THIRD MONTH 7 Sivan Fifty days later	Leviticus 23:15-22
Feast of Trumpets *(Rosh Hashanah)* STARTS THIRD SEASON	Exodus Chapter 40	God indwells the Tabernacle	SEVENTH MONTH 1 Tishri	Leviticus 23:23-25 Numbers 29:1-6
Day of Atonement *(Yom Kippur)*	(The first year every Israelite repented at the door of the taberna-cle.)	High Priest sprinkles blood on Mercy Seat (started second year)	10 Tishri	Leviticus 23:26-32 Numbers 29:7-11
Feast of Tabernacles *(Sukkot or Succoth)*	Leviticus 8:30 – 9:24	God's glory and fire appears, forty years in tents, connected with latter harvest	15-23 Tishri	Leviticus 23:33-44 Numbers 29:12-40

The underlined feasts are the ones which name the season.

[9] Nisan is also called *Abib* (Exod. 13:4) or *Aviv*.

Let's briefly review the feasts through these dual intertwined themes of meaning. In redemptive terms, Jesus' death, burial, and resurrection fulfilled the first season of Passover exactly on the date of its celebration. **Jesus was and is *the* spotless Paschal Lamb** that took away the sin of the world so that eternal death might *pass over* every one that partakes of the provision of His shed blood. Jesus willingly gave up His life on the cross at the ninth hour, or 3 p.m. This was the exact time when the Paschal or Passover lambs were sacrificed for the Passover feast.

> **[A]nd the whole assembly of the congregation of Israel shall kill it** [Passover lamb] **in the evening. (Exod. 12:6b)**

The phrase "in the evening" literally means "between the evenings." Both noon and 6 p.m. were considered "evening," and 3 p.m. is between them. The great price our Lord paid is called the *mohar* meaning "the price of the bride." In Bible times the Hebrew wife was purchased and owned by her husband. The Hebrew word *beulah*, which is translated "wife," literally means "*owned*." We were bought with a price; we are not *our* own (1 Cor. 6:19-20). We were bought with the incorruptible blood of Jesus (1 Pet. 1:18-19)! We are His!

Jesus was and is *the* Unleavened Bread. During the modern Jewish Passover Seder or dinner, there is a special pouch with three compartments holding three unleavened matzo crackers. Each cracker has several rows of holes in them. During the meal the Jewish participants accept these matzos as representing Abraham, Isaac, and Jacob. The middle one is always removed and broken in half. One half is then shared among all the family members participating, each eating a portion of it. The other half, called the *afikomen*, is hidden. At the conclusion of the meal, the children are encouraged to find the afikomen, and the one who does find it is rewarded with money or a special treat. In truth, these three matzos represent God the Father, God the

Son, and God the Holy Spirit. The middle one, the One made flesh (Jesus), was broken for us, bearing stripes on His back (rows) with nail-pierced feet and hands (holes). He was then hidden in the grave but found by all who believe with child-like faith, receiving the reward of eternal life through the remission of their sins. Upon resurrection, **Jesus also became *the* First Fruits** (1 Cor. 15:23) of all who would follow in the new birth. He was the first of many brethren. **Jesus totally fulfilled the first feast season of Passover for us.**

The New Covenant (promised by Jesus during the Last Supper or Passover Seder) is similar to the Old Covenant of Mt. Sinai. It too is a marriage covenant, or *brit.* A brit requires that blood must flow. In a natural marriage covenant, the blood flows at the initial sexual union of husband and wife. For the Old Covenant, Moses sprinkled Israel with the blood of animals, but in our covenant, the better covenant, the Covenant Initiator and Groom shed His very own sinless blood. In the marriage covenant meal, there was also a special cup of the covenant called the *Birkat Erusin.* Both the bride and groom share this cup of wine symbolizing a joint life. During the Passover Seder, Jesus took that cup after supper saying, "This cup is the New Testament [Covenant] in My blood" (1 Cor. 11:25). Jesus and the original bride in preparation partook of that cup together. Later, as He gave up His life on the cross, Jesus said, "It is finished." This phrase comes from the Hebrew root *kalah,* which means "to complete, make perfect or finish." The Hebrew word *kallah* means "the perfect bride." Our dear Lord Jesus had the perfecting of His bride on His mind when He laid down His life for us. Romeo's *eros* passion for Juliet is but a fleeting shadow of the agape passion of Christ for us. He paid a great price by which to grant all of us to shine forth His radiant love and glory now and for all eternity, not just manage life until departure.

In Bible days, once a marriage proposal was sealed, the bridegroom would leave his beloved and go to his father's house to build a wedding chamber or *chadar* for her. During this time, his bride was to prepare herself to go with him at his return for her. After His resurrection, Jesus ascended to His Father for that very purpose.

> **In my Father's house are many mansions: if *it* were not so, I would have told you. I go to prepare a place for you. And if I go and prepare a place for you, I will come again, and receive you unto myself; that where I am, *there* ye may be also. (John 14:2-3)**

We are in the days when the Bridegroom is taken away from us (Matt. 9:15). The passionate bride attentively and expectantly awaits His return. Along with the Spirit, the expectant bride says, "Come!" It is interesting that our original endowment of the Spirit is but the "earnest of the Spirit" (2 Cor. 1:22) or the pledge of His love, much like an engagement ring placed upon a bride's finger. As we begin to awaken to our role as His holy bride, that pledge will sparkle in far greater intensity, an eye-catching brilliancy before a world in grim darkness. Our Lord fulfilled Passover to bring us into covenant with Him. We recall His Passion in affectionate remembrance annually during the Passover (Easter) season and every time we partake of the sacrament of communion (1 Cor. 11:23-26, AMP). Jesus went before us as the First Fruits in resurrection, and He will raise us up too in that day yet to come! Our lives must manifest this work done for us.

The second feast season, Pentecost, was seemingly fulfilled with and through the church in Acts chapter 2. But actually, Pentecost is *not* finished! Hundreds of years after the original Pentecost at Mt. Sinai, the Lord foretold, through the prophet Joel, of two particular times in the future when the Holy Spirit would be poured out upon the earth.

> **Be glad then, ye children of Zion, and rejoice in the LORD your God: for he hath given you the former rain moderately, and he will cause to come down for you the rain, the former rain, and the latter rain in the first *month*. (JOEL 2:23)**

In agricultural terms, the former or early rains of Palestine were between mid-October to mid-November. These rains prepare the soil for the seed of the early harvest celebrated at Pentecost. Seed corresponds to birth. The Pentecost of Acts chapter 2 birthed the church. Like the original Pentecost of Mt. Sinai, there was a rushing wind, tongues of fire, and explosive growth in the church. But by Joel's foretelling, Acts 2 was only "the former rain in moderation" (Joel 2:23a), i.e., just enough to get the initial job done, which it did. The church was born: an infant bride of Christ.

Of course, God never intended for the move of His Spirit to dwindle and dissipate, but in His omniscience, He knew the infant bride of Christ would not maintain the flames, so He designed a far greater Pentecost at the end of two days or two thousand years. It was defined by Joel as "the former rain and the latter rain" together (Joel 2:23b). And this was confirmed by Hosea and further explained by Peter.

> **After two days will he revive us: in the third day he will raise us up, and we shall live in his sight. Then shall we know, *if* we follow on to know the LORD: his going forth *is* prepared as the morning; and he shall come unto us as the rain, as the latter and former rain *unto* the earth. (HOSEA 6:2-3)**

> **But, beloved, be not ignorant of this one *thing*, that one day *is* with the Lord as a thousand years, and a thousand**

years as one day. (2 Pet. 3:8)

We are quickly approaching the end of the second day (two thousand years) from the church's birth (not Jesus' birth). The fullness, or culmination, of Pentecost has begun. The attentive church will mature in Christ as she keeps this feast! Just as the former rain in the natural realm is far exceeded by the latter rain, so will the former rain of His Spirit (Acts chapter 2) be immensely overshadowed by His unrestrained and all pervasive former and latter rain of glory approaching us now.

The natural latter rain always precedes a far, far greater harvest too. So it will be in the spirit as well. Christ has planted His seed within each of us at our rebirth and we are to grow to His full stature or maturity in Christ especially in these end-days. All creation is waiting "for the manifestation of the sons of God" (Rom. 8:19) which in the Amplified Bible says is "revealing, the disclosing of their sonship." A "child" (in Greek, *teknon*), means "a product of birth"; but "son," *huis*, means "one who makes the fact of his or her relationship with God manifest in character and works." This greater outpouring of God's Spirit has already begun in numerous places such as Argentina, Brazil, and elsewhere to hasten our maturation as His bride from which will escalate a massive global harvest of lost souls! **This is the true final fulfilment of the second feast, Pentecost, by the Holy Spirit through the church before the return of our heavenly Groom for us.**

Finally, there is universal agreement that the third feast season has yet to be fulfilled. This final season includes three feasts: the Feast of Trumpets, the Day of Atonement, and finally, the Feast of Tabernacles. In ancient Israel, the father of the bridegroom determined the time the groom returned for his bride. Jesus confirmed this concerning His own return when He said, "Of that day and that hour knoweth no man, no, not the angels which are in heaven, neither the Son, but the Father" (Mk. 13:32). Usually, the groom returned late at night, often at midnight, and stood at the outer perimeter of the village in which his bride lived to call her out unto himself with shouts and the blowing of the shofar or trumpet. The bride would adorn herself with jewels (Isaiah 61:10) and come out to meet him. He would then carry her away to the home he had prepared for them. Many theorize the future rapture as the fulfillment of the Feast of Trumpets, which means "the trumpets to awaken."

> **For this we say unto you by the word of the Lord, that we which are alive *and* remain unto the coming of the Lord shall not prevent them which are asleep. For the Lord himself shall descend from heaven with a shout, with the voice of the archangel, and with the trump of God: and the dead in Christ shall rise first: Then we which are alive *and* remain shall be caught up together with them in the clouds, to meet the Lord in the air: and so shall we ever be with the Lord. (1 Thess. 4:15-17)**

> **In a moment, in the twinkling of an eye, at the last trump: for the trumpet shall sound, and the dead shall be raised incorruptible, and we shall be changed. (1 Cor. 15:52)**

Since all the feasts start and end on two different days, sundown to sundown, no one will know the day nor the hour of His return. That is why the bride is instructed to keep the feasts and remain watchful in prayer. The watchful bride will not miss His coming.

Following the Feast of Trumpets (*Rosh Hashanah*) is the Day of Atonement (*Yom Kippur*). It is a day of deep affliction. It depicts well the future tribulation of natural Israel starting, perhaps chronologically, on these feast days and then ending during the same feast days seven years later. However, while judgment pours out on earth, the bride who had already made herself ready (Jew first, then Gentile) will be feasting those seven years with her Groom just as the ancient wedding feasts lasted seven days. And our banquet will far surpass even the banquets of *Ahasuerus* in Esther 1.

> **Let us be glad and rejoice, and give honour to him: for the marriage of the Lamb is come, and his wife hath made herself ready. And to her was granted that she should be arrayed in fine linen, clean and white: for the fine linen is the righteousness of saints. And he saith unto me, Write, Blessed are they which are called unto the marriage supper of the Lamb . . . (Rev. 19:7-9)**

During the marriage supper, the second cup of wine will seal the marriage covenant. This is the cup of which Jesus said, "I will not drink henceforth of this fruit of the vine, until that day when I drink it new with you in my Father's kingdom" (Matt. 26:29). He is waiting for His beloved bride. Together we will rejoice!

In redemptive terms, the Feast of Tabernacles is ultimately seen as the future day when God, the Father, returns to a gloriously renovated earth that He might tabernacle with men once again after the millennial reign of Christ (the third day of Hosea 6:2). As it was in the beginning, so it shall be in the end.

> **Then I heard a mighty voice from the throne and I perceived its distinct words, saying, See! The abode of God is with men, and He will live [encamp, tent] among them; and they shall be His people, and God shall personally be with them and be their God. (Rev. 21:3)**

The word translated "live," "tent," and "encamp" is the Greek *skenoo*. Skenoo is the same word used for God's residing presence in the Tabernacle of the Congregation. It represents the grand finale when God the Father returns to dwell among men here on earth. Believing mankind (both Jew and Gentile) will live, rule, and reign with Him in Paradise on earth forever!

But that's not all! There is a third layer of revelation within these feasts. It is very important to the end-day church.

3. **The progressive union of Christ and His bride as witnessed by the world before Jesus' return in a distinct end-day period of time.**

It is the closing phase of the "two days" (two thousand years) since Acts chapter 2, the birth of the church. The bride is awaking to be made ready by keeping these feasts (not by the letter of the law but by His Spirit) until the two (Christ and His bride) become one. We are to be one in soul as well as spirit, one in character and in works, and one in manifest splendor and glory throughout the earth. It is an ever-increasing display of our union through escalating signs and wonders and miracles throughout the globe. Why? Because our Groom is so in love with His bride; He yearns to bring her home in splendor. Together we will start to celebrate our eternal union at the marriage supper! This third level of revelation presently unfolding is the theme of this book. So, *get ready*—He is coming for us soon!

CHAPTER 3

LEAVE AND CLEAVE

> **The feast of unleavened bread shalt thou keep: seven days thou shalt eat unleavened bread, as I commanded thee . . . (Exod. 34:18a)**

> **Therefore shall a man leave his father and his mother, and shall cleave unto his wife . . . (Gen. 2:24a)**

The first feast **the bride is to keep is the Feast of Unleavened Bread**, which, for Israel, begins with Passover and ends with First Fruits. It is a seven-day feast season. Seven means "complete" or "mature." In New Covenant terms, it is the span of our lifetime in Christ from our new birth to our passage to heaven. It denotes our completion or maturation while yet on earth. And it is to be unleavened. Jesus equated leaven with the religious doctrine or mindset of the Pharisees and Sadducees, calling them an adulterous generation (Matt. 16:4), so *un*leavened bread conveys the absence of spiritual adultery and more. For the Israelites of Moses' day, the leaven (or yeast) was removed from their bread at Passover when the blood of the Passover lambs was applied to the doorposts of their homes, and thereby, they were delivered from the death grip of Egypt. The next day they physically *left* Egypt (a type of the world system or worldly spirit). And though they traveled seven days with unleavened bread, they still hid the real leaven (Egypt) within their hearts. That spiritual leaven would eventually divide many hearts toward Jehovah God.

Our Creator, our Grand Designer, had already established in the marriage covenant that a man should *leave* his father and mother and *cleave* to his wife that the two shall become one (Gen. 2:24). Leave and cleave. Both are critically important. Any union of marriage is endangered should one spouse refuse to emotionally *leave* his or her parents and *cleave* to his or her mate. So it is no surprise that in Jehovah's marriage contract, He included Exodus 20:1-7, which are the first three commandments or obligations of the wife, Israel, to her Husband as written in their marriage ketubah.

> **And God spake all these words, saying, I *am* the LORD thy God, which have brought thee out of the land of Egypt, out of the house of bondage. Thou shalt have no other gods before me. Thou shalt not make unto thee any graven image, or any likeness of *any thing* . . . Thou shalt not bow down thyself to them, nor serve them: for I the LORD thy God *am* a jealous God . . . Thou shalt not take the name of the LORD thy God in vain; for the LORD will not hold him guiltless that taketh his name in vain. (Exod. 20:1-4a, 5, 7)**

Jehovah was declaring to His beloved something like, "I am your Lord. My power rescued you out of Egypt and My power will keep Egypt out of you *if* you cleave *only* to Me. Thou shalt have no other lovers besides Me, your Husband. You are My wife, so don't mess around with Egypt because I do get very jealous." Moses later repeatedly advised the second generation Israelites to *cleave* to Jehovah throughout the book of Deuter-

[10] The only exceptions were Joshua and Caleb, who did cleave to the Lord God.

onomy so they would not make same mistake of their parents[10] who did *not cleave* and died in the wilderness (Deut. 4:4, 10:20, 11:22, 13:4, 30:20).

How many men are going to marry a woman who is faithful 364 days of the year? A real husband is not about to share his wife with anyone, anytime, for any reason. And so it is with Yahweh. Moses and the Israelites did leave Egypt, but only Moses and a few others were making themselves ready by passionately cleaving to God. The majority of Israel kept their cool distance, and within a few months of the wedding ceremony, slid right into spiritual adultery. What does this mean for us? Jesus shed His blood and purchased our deliverance almost two thousand years ago, and when we were born again, we each said, "I do," and were wed to the King of kings. Our Groom immediately delivered us from sin, eternal death, Satan, and the power of this world. And Jesus, as with any groom, desires and rightfully expects our *total* affection and attention as His eternal, beloved bride.

Now, women will relate to this the best. Remember those romantic fairytales we loved when we were young? The dashing, chivalrous, handsome prince rescues the princess in distress, kisses her, and carries her off with him to live together happily ever after. Then you grew up, got married, and figured out that it wasn't all true. But it is true! It's just that in this sin-infested realm, this truth can never be purely and fully demonstrated in natural terms by sin-stained humans. But *Jesus is our perfect Prince!* He rescued us from the dragon, Satan. And He will soon carry us away to live with Him forever in heavenly bliss. Right now Jesus is awakening us with a kiss to intimacy with Him, for He *is* the lover of our souls. Through the Holy Spirit, He is standing at the door of our hearts ever knocking (Rev. 3:20). He desires to woo us, court us, and romance us as His cherished, beautiful bride. He is totally in love with us!

God created *romance* and *passion*. They are wedding gifts for the Son and His bride. Mankind's natural marriage covenant received a resembling portion but only because that union symbolizes the *true holy union* of Christ and His bride (and Jehovah and Israel). That is why we are drawn to romantic movies. It was and still is Jesus we all yearn for. The world has perverted romance and passion and capitalized on them both, but the Father created them for a divine purpose, i.e., for us to fall madly in love with His Son and forever *cleave only* to Him. Jesus craves to demonstrate His burning love for us, seize our hearts, and flame our passion for Him alone. *That* is personal revival! It is our return to our first love (Rev. 2:4). There is no love life that compares with true intimacy with our Lord Jesus through the Holy Spirit. It was purchased for us with His blood. It belongs to the entire body of Christ. But only those believers who respond to His invitation and pursue this magnificent fellowship of love will experience it and its fruit as the bride being made ready.

We must be careful about whom or what we cling to. Anything that diminishes our attentiveness and affections toward Jesus is an idol or false lover. While false religions are most prone to shackle the lost, the spirit of Egypt, or the worldly spirit, is the most aggressive false lover diligently aspiring to ensnare the saints. It is continually vying for our affection to draw us away from Jesus. It pursues our souls night and day, and if we are not watchful, the world can suddenly whisk us away into spiritual adultery just as it did the majority of newlywed Israel. Certainly we all have been with unfaithful Israel and the five foolish virgins at some time or another in our Christian walk. I know I have.

> **Ye adulterers and adulteresses, know ye not that the friendship of the world is enmity with God? whosoever**

therefore will be a friend of the world is the enemy of God. Do ye think that the scripture saith in vain, The spirit that dwelleth in us lusteth to envy? (JAMES 4:4-5)

For Israel, the spiritual adultery was the worship of the golden calf, and later, many other heathen gods. For Christian believers in developed nations, it is primarily friendship or fondness with the world. Our Lord is divinely jealous of any time that we squander on this other lover. When a man deeply loves a woman, his heart burns if she even momentarily appears attracted to another. Even worse, he is deeply hurt by her declining devotion toward him. If we are not careful, worldly passions will cool down our zeal for the Lord. Jesus loves us dearly. He proved that when He left heaven for earth to die a brutal death for our ransom and dowry. Even now, He ever lives to intercede for us. What total devotion He has toward us! Can we give Him any less in return?

Right now we are *in* the world. That we cannot help. We just cannot be *of* the world or have the world *govern* us. Any amount of worldliness is a divided heart, a heart not exclusively in love with Jesus. The apostle of love, John, understood this truth and urgently compelled all the church to leave the world.

Love not the world, neither the things that are in the world. If any man love the world, the love of the Father is not in him. For all that is in the world, the lust of the flesh, and the lust of the eyes, and the pride of life, is not of the Father, but is of the world. And the world passeth away, and the lust thereof: but he that doeth the will of God abideth for ever. (1 JOHN 2:15-17)

The outpouring of God's Spirit in these last days has been called by many "the Father's love." It is decisively clear in this Scripture that by our romancing the world, we could miss recognizing and flowing with this outpouring. *Things* are not wrong in and of themselves—they are only wrong when they take precedence over or exceed our love and attention for our Lord. In other words, it all depends on how they compare to Jesus in the scale and balance of our affections. We must frequently examine our hearts making a regular comparative analysis.

Take, for instance, the lust of the flesh. When we gratify the desires of the body and overindulge in something like chocolate, it is *only* lust because we overindulge on something *other than Him.* Self-seeking is also wrong, but only because we are seeking someone (our self) other than Him, pleasing self instead of pleasing Him. Lust is also exalting our comfort over our effort to be with Him or do His will. There is nothing wrong with comfort. Both our heavenly Father and our Groom want us to be blessed. He sent the Comforter for the difficult times. But a comfortable inward church, a church satisfied with her own salvation and not compelled to reach outward to the lost whom He also loves, is, in truth, lusting after the flesh.

Likewise, the lust of the eyes occurs when our attention and meditations are captivated by things in the natural realm rather than the things of the Spirit—things that interest our Lord and Savior. The lust of the eyes is the relentless pursuit of luxury and possessions *instead of* an extravagant pursuit of Christ as lover and Lord. If we pursue Him and His Kingdom, all the things we need will come (Matt. 6:33). What groom doesn't bear gifts for the bride who is consumed with love for him? The lust of the eyes is also going after things we don't really need rather than sharing our excess with those in need whom He also loves. Our choices are either toward Him or toward self and the world.

The pride of life or pride embodies the most hideous similitude to the world mindset. Again, it implies a life out of balance by God's standards. The pride of life is exalting our own reasoning above the thoughts and ways of God and trusting in our own ability, strength, or works rather than acknowledging our total and utter dependency on Him. It is most evident (at least to others) when we think too highly of ourselves instead of focusing our eyes upon Him and esteeming Him above self. Pride is also seeking our own priorities rather than His. Most of the time, it is not so much the issue of making the wrong choice but the fact that we did not even make inquiry of Him concerning His direction and will in our choice.

Spiritual adultery with the world is nothing new. It originated with Lucifer before the throne of God, and Satan swiftly passed it on in the Garden of Eden. When Eve saw that the tree was "good for food" and pleasing to the taste—that was the lust of the flesh. When Eve saw the fruit as "pleasant to her eye," the lust of the eyes took charge of her. When it was "a tree to be desired to make one wise," the pride of life (Gen. 3:6) took root within her. Adam (who was there with her the whole time) and Eve fell to the spirit of this world. It became their god, their false lover. Their newly fallen sin nature perfectly reflected the very nature of the worldly spirit himself (Satan).

On the other hand, Jesus, who loved *only* the Father, considered *only* the Father, and pleased *only* the Father, was also tempted in these same three ways while in the wilderness. Yet He did not sin. The temptation to turn stones into bread was the lust of the flesh. It did not successfully entice Him. He refused to provide Himself food even though His physical flesh screamed for nourishment. Instead, our Groom chose to wait on the Father's provision and the Father's timing for that provision. Satan's enticing offer of all the world's kingdoms and their beautiful accessories was an embodiment of the lust of the eyes. Again, Jesus refused. He chose to wait for His Father's kairos timing when "the kingdoms of this world become the Kingdoms of our Lord and of His Christ" (Rev. 11:15). Satan's ploy for an instant and sensational following after an uninjured leap from the temple demonstrated the pride of life. And Jesus refused again. He would not circumvent His suffering unto obedience, which was the Father's way, the way of the cross.

Again, the worldly mindset is likened to the leaven of the Pharisees and Sadducees. The day Jesus warned His disciples of their doctrine, the Pharisees and Sadducees had come to Him to tempt Him just as had Satan in the wilderness. They tempted Him to perform a spectacular miracle to attest His divine authority (Matt. 16:1, AMP). And they were not the only ones whose minds were deluded by the world. Some of those who had witnessed the miracle of multiplication later tempted Jesus in Capernaum to multiply bread when there was no longer a fainting, hungering multitude afar off from villages and towns (Jn. 6:30-41). Right after Peter recognized Jesus as Messiah (Matt. 16:16-18), he tempted Him to avoid the cross (Matt. 16:22-23) and others later tried to lure Jesus to come down from the cross (Matt. 27:40). Overall, the worldly mindset tried to seduce Christ to exploit and use His delegated authority and power at His own will, benefit, and timing instead of the Father's. It is a deceptive urge to *make something happen* instead of waiting upon the leading of the Spirit and timing of the Father. But in all these temptations Jesus did not fail, and He encourages us by saying, "Be of good cheer, I have overcome the world; so will you, My beautiful bride."

How can we tell if we are *of* the world? It can be difficult. The prophet Joel admonishes us that worldliness causes a semblance of drunkenness or stupor. When one is drunk, one is unaware of the real danger of one's condition and numb to its warning signs. Only the Comforter can sober our inebriated soul and reveal to us the true state of our hearts. Joel clearly indicates, however, some warning signs: spiritual dryness, lack of joy, lack of revelation, lack of vision, lack of heaven-sent provision, sickness, scarcity of the gifts of the Spirit, and a meager harvest of souls. That list aptly describes the vast majority of the church in North America at this time. James' exhortation for the adulterous church is to "draw nigh to Him (cleave) and He will draw nigh to you" (James 4:7) i.e., empower you to *leave* the world. James goes on to write: "humble yourselves in the sight of the Lord, He will lift you up" (James 4:10). We draw nigh to Him by seeking His face, His presence, and His instruction. Humbling our souls often requires fasting.

In the summer of 1997, I was exceptionally dry. I was frustrated and hearing meagerly from the Lord. My joy level was approaching empty. I knew something was drastically wrong, but I didn't want to admit that my dance card wasn't filled up with Christ alone. I had been dancing a few tunes with the world. Fortunately, I got desperate enough to request a fast. Fasting shakes us to sobriety so we may correctly see the condition of our soul and hear once again the beat of our Father's heart. Fasting does not change God. Instead, it shatters our stubborn resistance and allows us to line up with Him and His purposes for our lives. The particular fast He gave me was five days on water from Saturday, July 5, through Wednesday, July 9, in trying and uncomfortable conditions away from home, sleeping on a floor in heat and humidity with limited bathroom privileges. Little did I know that He was purposefully preparing me for an eighteen-day mission trip in Argentina where I would again experience trying conditions a few months later.

God got right down to business with me. The first evening of my fast, the Lord led me to two Scriptures: 2 Corinthians 6:1-10 and Revelation 3:14-21. The apostle Paul, like Moses, is compared to the chaste, pure, awakened bride of Christ, while the Laodicean church models the spiritually adulterous church.

Listen to the heart of the bride. Note the in(s) and by(s) and as(s).

> **We then, as workers together *with him,* beseech you also that ye receive not the grace of God in vain. (For he saith, I have heard thee in a time accepted, and in the day of salvation have I succoured thee: behold, now is the accepted time; behold, now *is* the day of salvation.) Giving no offence in any *thing,* that the ministry be not blamed: But in all *things* approving ourselves as the ministers of God, in much patience, in afflictions, in necessities, in distresses, In stripes, in imprisonments, in tumults, in labours, in watchings, in fastings; By pureness, by knowledge, by long suffering, by kindness, by the Holy Ghost, by love unfeigned, By the word of truth, by the power of God, by the armour of righteousness on the right hand and on the left, By honour and dishonour, by evil report and good report: as deceivers, and *yet* true; As unknown, and *yet* well known; as dying, and, behold, we live; as chastened, and not killed; As sorrowful, yet alway rejoicing; as poor, yet making many rich; as having nothing, and yet possessing all *things.* (2 Cor. 6:1-10)**

As a minister of reconciliation and ambassador for Christ, Paul found himself "in" many difficult and trying situations. He was in the world, a world resisting his message of truth. The next phrases beginning with "by" describe the attitude and means through which Paul passed these trials. He emphasizes the power and grace of God that enables any true disciple to live above difficult circumstances while maintaining the character of Christ. Next, each phrase beginning with "as" conveys Paul's reputation as assessed by the opposing standards of the world versus our holy Lord's standards. To the world, this traveling preacher and tentmaker was poor. But to God, Paul and the awakened believers traveling with him were wealthy in spirit and making many others rich as well. Paul was in the world but certainly not of it.

Unfortunately, we are often brainwashed to think like the world. To reverse this requires that our brain be washed with the water of His Word to separate us *from* the world. How different Paul was in comparison with the Laodicean church!

> **And unto the angel of the church of the Laodiceans write; These *things* saith the Amen, the faithful and true witness, the beginning of the creation of God; I know thy works, that thou art neither cold nor hot: I would thou wert cold or hot. So *then* because thou art lukewarm, and neither cold nor hot, I will spue thee out of my mouth. Because thou sayest, I am rich, and increased with goods, and have need of nothing; and knowest not that thou art wretched, and miserable, and poor, and blind, and naked: I counsel thee to buy of me gold tried in the fire, that thou mayest be rich; and white raiment, that thou mayest be clothed, and *that* the shame of thy nakedness do not appear; and anoint thine eyes *with* eyesalve, that thou mayest see. (Rev. 3:14-18)**

The Laodicean church *thought* they were rich and in need of nothing, but they were sadly mistaken. The deception came when they measured their abundance by the world's standards and not by God's. Most of the modern church of North America falls into this disreputable category. It *appears* that we (the church of the USA) are blessed. We have all this stuff. (It is all right for us to have stuff as long as the stuff doesn't have us!) But Jesus says that worldly treasure is not the heavenly measure of wealth and prosperity. In Jehovah Jireh's (our Provider's) economy, we are *poor* when we are deficient in the things of God. We are *blind* when we lack revelatory vision. We are *naked* when we are not clothed with His glory and displaying the power of the Most High. We cannot romance Jesus with a lukewarm heart.

A betrothed maiden without passion is not a true bride. Her heart is divided. Her eye is not single. If we have one foot in the world and one foot in Christ, a deep marital fellowship will fail to develop. But there is a way of escape for those of us who have straddled that fence.

We can successfully *leave* the world. Of course, first we must truly desire it and then recognize that only in God's ability can we accomplish it, for it requires true heart-rending repentance.

> **As many as I love, I rebuke and chasten: be zealous therefore, and repent. (Rev. 3:19)**

Fasting often prepares us for something only the Holy Spirit can do, that is, initiate true repentance. By His Spirit, God reveals to us our own hearts and convinces us of our sin. There is a false repentance that leads to death, but true repentance leads to life. Judas' repentance led to death; Peter's to life. The condemnation of the devil or religious spirit never produces life. There is never a resolution. It is like a trap with no way out. But when the Holy Spirit convicts or convinces us, He immediately leads us *to* and *through* repentance, and the weight of sin is instantly lifted off and gone (1 John 1:9). **True repentance is the means by which we can leave the world.** Then, once again, our bread or life becomes *unleavened*. That first night in that hot July, I broke down in tears of repentance before my redeeming Savior for all *my* many flirtations and entanglements with the world. The weight of sin lifted off me, and I was free and bursting with joy again.

But it must not end there! Often, after sincere repentance, we return to that same adultery the next day or week or month like a dog to its vomit. Leaving *alone* is not enough to overcome the world. It is in the *cleaving* to our heavenly Groom that we are empowered to stay clear of worldliness and *remain* unleavened.

How do we *cleave*? It is simple. Jesus unfolds it to us in the next verse.

> **Behold, I stand at the door, and knock: if any *man* hear my voice, and open the door, I will come in to him, and will sup with him, and he with me. (Rev. 3:20)**

Sharing a meal in biblical times represented intimate fellowship, and every meal began with the breaking of bread. It was in the breaking of bread that our Lord's Emmaus-bound disciples recognized Him. Bread also represents revelation, which is another delightful portion of our personal revival.

Intimate fellowship along with obedience are the means by which we cleave to Jesus. As we give more and more of our consideration and devotion to our Lord and our time and fellowship with Him, He becomes foremost in our lives, and the power of this world loses its hold on us. How is this possible? It is possible because of the Holy Spirit. His presence in us is ever ready and capable to dispossess the spirit of the world from our lives at our beckoning.

> [G]**reater is he** [Holy Spirit] **that is in you, than he that is in the world. (1 John 4:4b)**

The *he that is in the world* is the spirit of the world or worldly spirit. As we *cleave* to Jesus, we are empowered by the Greater One, the Holy Spirit in us, to not fall back into the world as did the children of Israel. We *can* live unleavened. And there is even another greater benefit to living *in* but not *of* the world. To the degree of our liberation *from* the world, we are empowered by the Spirit of God to set free other captives *of* the world! But to the degree the bride is sleeping with the world, she will be powerless to deliver those lost within the world. We will love the one we worship. We will love the one with whom we spend time. We will love the one upon which we meditate. Let it be Christ our

Lord and none other.

When the Israelites left Egypt, they were all healthy. "There was not one feeble person among their tribes" (Ps. 105:37b), and God declared Himself to them as "the LORD that healeth thee" (Exod. 15:26b). He wills to be our Healer today. But we *too* must leave Egypt. We must leave the world's provision and portions of food and cleave to *God's* provision and choices just as did Daniel and his three Israelite companions. For some, He may require a fasted lifestyle or occasional short fasts. For others, He may only require sound nutrition or moderation. Whatever He desires, we must obey. In modern terminology, this is self-discipline. In biblical terminology, it is crucifying the flesh.

When the Israelites left Egypt, they were also wealthy "with silver and gold" (Ps. 105:37a). If we are going to be wealthy, we too must leave Egypt behind. We must *leave* the self-centeredness and the world's financial system of impulse buying, charging, and borrowing behind. Instead, we must *cleave* unto God's laws of financial blessing: faithfully giving tithes, offerings, and alms (to the poor), while living within our means and patiently waiting for our sure reward in His kairos timing. It is a holy contentment and trust in Him. And like the Israelites, we also leave Egypt every time we choose God's will over our own. Thereby, we honor Him and conquer the pride of life. As long as we exalt Him above ourselves *to ourselves,* we will walk in true humility. This Father does know best, and He knows best *every* time. Victory calls for less reasoning and more listening. All His commandments are for our good, and if we will submit our choices to Him, neither pride, nor the lust of the eyes, nor the lust of the flesh will ever have a death grip upon us or place within us.

This is a lifelong process, and, in this process, "weeping may endure for a night, but joy comes in the morning" (Ps. 30:5).

It is the working out of the salvation of our souls in fear and in trembling (Phil. 2:12). It is our soul's sanctification, separation from the world, a setting apart of the bride without spot or wrinkle for her Beloved. And it is worth the time and effort. Hear our Lord and King's magnificent promise to those who overcome the lukewarm attitude and spiritual adultery with the world or other gods by cleaving to Jesus.

> **To him that overcometh will I grant to sit with me in my throne, even as I also overcame, and am set down with my Father in his throne. (Rev. 3:21)**

Who but the holy bride of Christ should sit down on the right side of heaven's Bridegroom! Our intimate knowledge of and communion with our Lord and the manifested presence of Christ *in* us and *with* us and *through* us will validate our having overcome the world. These overcomers are His bride made ready, and our Groom will manifest our holy union before the nations of the world before His return for us. We will walk side by side in great splendor in these last days just as He did with them in the former days. And as marvelous as that is, it is but a foretaste of our joint rulership in the millenniums to come! ***Leave* the world by *cleaving* to Jesus!** We can do this in His strength. Let's keep the feasts.

CHAPTER 4

ENTERING HIS REST

Six days thou shalt work, but on the seventh day thou shalt rest: in earing time and in harvest thou shalt rest. (EXOD. 34:21)

Remember the sabbath day, to keep it holy. Six days shalt thou labour, and do all thy work: But the seventh day is the sabbath of the LORD thy God: *in it* thou shalt not do any work, thou, nor thy son, nor thy daughter, thy manservant, nor thy maidservant, nor thy cattle, nor thy stranger that is within thy gates: For *in* six days the LORD made heaven and earth, the sea, and all that in them is, and rested the seventh day: wherefore the LORD blessed the sabbath day, and hallowed it. (EXOD. 20:8-11)

Keeping the Sabbath or Shabbat is one of the ten marital pledges of Israel to her Husband, Jehovah. She was instructed to refrain from physical labor one day a week, the seventh day or Saturday. Like Jehovah (Gen. 2:2) she was to rest. Her obedience was originally tested and proven in the gathering of manna (Exod. 16:30).

And he said unto them, The sabbath was made for man, *and* not man for the sabbath: (MARK 2:27)

For both Israel and the church, the Sabbath is a gift—a wedding gift—from the Groom to His beloved. It is intended to bless and benefit us. "Jesus is Lord of the Sabbath" and our keeping it is evidence of our union with Him. It is not just taking a day off from work to gather in worship. It is more.

> **There remaineth therefore a rest to the people of God. For he that is entered into his rest, he also hath ceased from his own works, as God *did* from his. Let us labour therefore to enter into that rest, lest any *man* fall after the same example of unbelief. (Heb. 4:9-11)**

As Christians, our pledge as bride to Groom is a pledge of ***resting* in Him**, a lifestyle of trust or faith in Christ our Lord in our day-to-day walk within an anxious, fear-ridden world. We are to cease from depending our own labors or physical efforts[11], our understanding, and our ability, and look solely and wholly to Christ in whatever the assignment or circumstance of our life. True *rest* is liberating. It primarily frees us to seek His face rather than His hands.

To seek His face means we desire to know and fellowship with Him. To seek His hands means to yearn for what He can provide or do for us. Unfortunately, many of our prayers are a monotony of petitions, endless requests, and continual naggings for "I want-ums." Consider this in terms of natural maturation. Little children want everything; they ask for everything. For their sake, their parents make sure they don't *get* everything. And as they *do* mature, they begin to notice their parents as unique persons who love them and begin to prefer their parents as individuals over the niceties that they can give them. Ap-

[11] That does not mean we do no work. The apostle Paul made it clear that those who will not work, will not eat (2 Thess. 3:10). This is more an attitude of rest in Christ, regardless of our activity, and will actually prosper all proper business and activities.

proaching full maturity, they respect and honor their parents. Their selfish demands have ceased, or at least, diminished. They wish, out of love, to please and give of themselves and maintain enduring fellowship with their parents. So it is for us and our Lord. Seeking His face is focusing on Him as a person and especially delighting in His manifest presence. Generally, we most effectively get to know someone when we limit our talking and increase our listening. Spiritual intimacy grows as we lay aside our own immediate desires, personal agendas, and preconceived needs, and let Him initiate and handle the matters of our life while listening for His words to brighten our path in life (Ps. 119:105) and receive His affirmation. This is focusing on Him with quiet attentiveness like Mary at His feet and John upon His breast. Maturity and intimacy are signs of true love.

How many young women asked their intended for a list of his assets and liabilities and his five, ten, and twenty year projected goals before they were married? None that I know of. As a bride, you just looked into his eyes and smiled that silly smile. You didn't give a thought as to how he would provide for you. You simply trusted him to supply in his ability and timing. And that, by the way, is true submission. **True submission is *rest*.** The bride of Christ must enter this rest.

> **Likewise, ye younger, submit yourselves unto the elder. Yea, all *of you* be subject one to another, and be clothed with humility: for God resisteth the proud, and giveth grace to the humble. Humble yourselves therefore under the mighty hand of God, that he may exalt you in due time: (1 Pet. 5:5-6)**

How do we humble ourselves? Fasting, sometimes. But always by "casting all our care upon Him" for He rightly cares for us (1 Pet. 5:7). Submission to Jesus is truly *resting* in Him—His ability, His wisdom, His leadership, His provision, and His timing.

If we permit Jesus to handle the details of our life, then we are free to pursue sweet fellowship with Him. Honor Him. Respect Him. Everything is His. He is well able to manage our lives without our assistance. If we make loving our Lord our focus, He will tie up all the ends, put everything in place, and make all things work together for our good. He will fill us with His unconditional love, restore our souls, reaffirm us, and renew us until His life and love just naturally (and supernaturally) pour out from within us upon those around us, lost or saved. We don't have to work up anything. The ball is in His court. He calls the shots. Even revival is His. We can't rush it. We can't make it happen. The best thing we can do for ourselves, other believers, and the lost is to stay madly in love with Jesus. Evangelism and ministry will happen spontaneously. After all, when two love each other, the children just come by spiritual birth and heavenly adoption. Jesus loves us because the Father loves us, and He loves the Father. We will truly love each other and the lost when we love them because of our love for our Lord!

Entering our Lord's *rest* was definitely not an easy paradigm shift for me. I had been a focused, performance-minded, workaholic, man-pleasing over-achiever most of my life. But He gently drew me to seek His face. I began to see myself in private prayer as a waiter standing attentively beside His table. Once I received His order, I would act on it. It was easy and a joy. If He wanted me to lie on my face, I'd lie on my face. If He wanted me to dance, I'd dance. If He wanted me to do warfare, I'd enter in, and whatever the form of prayer I engaged in would be anointed because *He* initiated it. One of the keys toward rest is praying in the spirit. We give ourselves a rest when we avoid praying only from our understanding. Unless it is prophetic, there is no point. We are not in charge, He is. We don't even have to decide what to pray. Isaiah tells us that it is in the stammering lips—praying in the spirit (1 Cor. 14:14) or praying the Word that we find true rest (Isaiah 28:11-12, AMP). So throw out your requests and your agendas; wait on God. It's the precious *rest* He purchased for us.

Despite all His wonderful tutoring on rest, I often slipped back into my own striving and works. That is our carnal nature and religious training. One particular time, God gave me a strong impression that lasted for several days and then a dream to guide me back to *rest*.

> **IMPRESSION: For a few days now, I have felt as though I am in a very cold blizzard and cannot find my way out. I greatly desire just to lie down and sleep, but I know that means I will die.**

My outlook of this impression was that I must not give in. I interpreted it as a demonic attack and concluded that I had better fight with all my might. Do, do, do, do, do, do. The next day I was at a local public library where He spoke to my heart a word concerning my destiny. His hand came heavily upon me. I began to melt as His manifest presence of glory draped over me. I awkwardly managed to maneuver myself home, crawl up the stairs, and fling myself upon the bed. The remainder of that afternoon and all that night, His glory weighed upon me until I awoke early the next morning from a dream.

> **DREAM: I was wrestling for my life with a man I knew was stronger than me. He had a gun, and I struggled to keep out of the aim of its fire. Then I felt something and realized the barrel was pressed to my side. I thought, *I'm ready to go home. Why struggle? Just die.***

I had decided to die. I awoke, not realizing until later that I had just relinquished my life cares and will back into the safe hands of my Lord. I had reentered His *rest*.

It sounds very irresponsible to the natural mind, but it's not. Our obedience is the evidence of our faith even if it's doing nothing! (Not that everyone is called to do nothing even for a season. Most believers are called to their field of work, but even there, you can *rest* in Him.) All the men and women of faith in Hebrews chapter 11 received a promise from the Lord and *then* obediently moved on it. In response to their obedience, God brought forth the event or miraculous provision He had promised for *some*. But for *some others,* no fulfilment came in their lifetime. It came generations later. What great faith they had! That day the revelation "light" clicked on. I knew in my heart and not just my head that **ceasing from our own works was our keeping of the Sabbath**, a step that vitally maintains personal revival. The Lord Most High is searching for frail believers who will acknowledge their helplessness and dependency upon Him. He will pass over a million people to get to those who will lay down their lives to wait and listen and obey. Through rest, the bride will follow His leading into a deeper walk and a stronger anointing for greater works by which He will be glorified!

Gradually, the Lord drew our whole intercessory prayer group to rest. For several years, a group of ladies and myself had faithfully spent at least two mornings a week together in intercession for our congregation and a move of God's Spirit. Over the years we went through different prayer phases: first warfare, then prophetic intercession, and finally, worship intercession. In late summer one year, His presence would come upon us but no longer thrust us into warfare or reveal prophetic insights and wisdom or propel us to dance; it would merely serve to quiet us. We weren't praying, just soaking in His glory. For anyone who likes to *do*, this is very difficult. Be honest. Don't we assess our own value as well as the value of others by what we do rather than who we *are*? We *felt* irresponsible. We *felt* like we were letting people down. There were no burdens. Oh, occasionally He would anoint us to pray briefly, then down we would go again. Questions arose. Uncertainties mounted.

I sought the Lord. As I read my Bible, these verses seemed to leap off the page in explanation.

> **And the apostles gathered themselves together unto Jesus, and told him all things, both what they had done, and what they had taught. And he said unto them, Come ye yourselves apart into a desert place, and rest a while: for there were many coming and going, and they had no leisure so much as to eat. And they departed into a desert place by ship privately. (MARK 6:30-32)**

Jesus imparted to His disciples the principle of *rest*, **a rest from ministry.** When Luke the physician wrote his letter (the epistle of Acts) to Theophilus, he referred to his former treatise (the Gospel of Luke) as all that *Jesus began* both to *do* and *teach*. In other words, everything that Jesus *did* and *taught* during His earthly ministry was just the beginning. He mentored His disciples so they would continue to do and teach likewise but also *rest*. Unfortunately, we put so much emphasis on *doing* and *teaching*, we sometimes overlook the *resting*. Jesus regularly spent lavish time in private fellowship with His Father. Sometimes it was very early in the morning. Sometimes it was late at night or throughout the night. It was in these times of rest and intimate communion with the Father that He was infused with inner strength by the Holy Spirit. The outflow of this rest was the very means by which Jesus miraculously ministered to mankind. He was drawing from the resources of heaven deposited within Him in rest.

There is also a **rest in ministry.** In the fall of 1998, I sensed from the Lord that I was to speak at a breakfast meeting of Baltimore pastors and intercessors. But I wasn't even invited, yet alone scheduled to speak. Somehow, at the last minute, I was invited to the planning committee meeting. When permitted, I briefly but passionately shared my heart concerning a citywide vision. Nothing seemed to happen. No one seemed to respond. I felt pressured to express myself some more on the matter, but deep within, the Lord spoke to me: "If you *make* it happen, it is work. If you *let* it happen, it is rest." I kept my mouth shut. My attendance at the breakfast was now sure, but as yet, I still had no invitation to speak, but God turned that around in a couple of days. It was easy; it was rest. Resting in ministry or career is letting the Groom open the door for His bride. Ladies love it when our husbands or dates open the door of the car or restaurant for us. Let us permit our True Love to open some doors of ministry and career too! Rest in Jesus!

Of course, there came a time when I thought I should attend a particular meeting to which I *had* been invited. I kept asking God about it, but I wasn't hearing anything. It was Friday night and the meeting was scheduled for the next day. I spent the whole night listening for His voice because *I* wanted to go. In His great love for me, He spoke to me that night. His words reproved and corrected me, and taught me more about rest.

> **Word from the Lord: Want more than I permit. Want to go where you will. Want to be independent. But I say we are one and if you are submitted, you go only where I direct. You don't have to initiate anything. Good ideas are no good. God ideas are all that will do. Stop figuring it out. Let it unfold bit by bit, and let Me lead you. I can't dance with you if you are trying to lead. Did I tell you to go? No. Did you ask? Yes. That is *you* initiating. If I don't say go, don't ask. Stay, stay, stay put. Be, be, be with Me. Do, do, do only what I say. So, so, so I won't delay. This is meant to be a rest. Why do you continue to make it work? Have you not learned that if I do not initiate it, it will not work? It won't. There is no**

> **life in it. Now rest in Me. If I say go, go. If I say nothing, stay. It's not work. It's *rest*. Don't aim low to please men. Aim high, to please Me. Know that I know the end from the beginning. It is secure. Now rest.**

I wish I could honestly say that I have been perfectly at rest ever since, but I am still being processed.

Rest in God. It is such a wonderful gift! Amazingly, as believers, we can even rest from condemnation and sin! Our trying to live without sin in *our* strength and ability places us under the law. That's work. Rest is depending on His ability and His strength and His wonderful provision of grace. And His grace is not just to blot out repented sin. (Thank God it does.) But the magnificent power of His grace also enables us to live without sinning by resting in His strength to resist temptation. Romans 8:3b in the Amplified Bible says that Jesus' death "deprived [sin] of its power over all who accept that sacrifice." Why? So that we might fulfill the righteousness of the law, that is, walk upright like Him, walk without sinning but not in *our* ability, but in *His* ability. Jesus has overpowered sin and He offers His overpowering ability in us to us through His presence and grace.

He saved us from our sin nature once and for all, but He desires to continually save us from sinning each and every day, each and every hour, and each and every minute.

> **For by grace are ye saved through faith; and that not of yourselves: it is the gift of God. Not of works, lest any man should boast. (Eph. 2:8-9)**

This marital pledge was written *to* us and *for* us and applies day by day. It doesn't say, "By grace we *were* saved through

[12] This "are" is in the continual present tense. In the Weymouth translation a footnote adds: "The perfect tense implying 'and are now saved' *Aorist* vii."

faith." It says, "By grace we *are*[12] saved through faith." That "are" declares to us that His saving grace is available minute by minute, night and day, year in and year out. It is a place of great liberty and victory! The perfect Law Keeper lives in us. We merely step aside and permit Him to walk upright *through us, for us*. It is rest for our soul.

After recognizing this truth in Scripture, God permitted some illustrations in my life to imprint His Torah on my heart including rest from condemnation and rest while in temptation. False accusations from Satan are aimed to imprison our faith and steal our rest. But Jesus purchased for us a **rest *from* condemnation** for "there is therefore now no condemnation to them which are in Christ Jesus, who walk not after the flesh, but after the Spirit" (Rom. 8:1). One particular night after teaching, the Lord instructed me to pray for fresh fire for those attending my teaching series. This was something my pastor had encouraged me to do, but I had previously shied away from it. As I invited members to come forward for prayer, my pastor also came and began to pray with a few people. Then I noticed that he slipped away while I continued to minister for some time. Later that night the Accuser accused me of dishonoring my pastor. I had a wonderful pastor, and I took this very seriously. Even though the Lord had already given me a "well done" high-five, I sided with Satan's thought and went to sleep distraught. Have you ever done that? I bet you have.

The next morning I awoke in the loving presence of the Lord, but I was still upset. I said, "How can You love me after what I did," now *accusing myself*. He assured me that I had done no wrong, but I didn't receive it. Imagine that! I know better than God! In actuality I had believed my feelings over God's Truth! I believed the opinion of my soul over the knowledge of my spirit. I then made a very true statement, but I meant it as an argument. I said, "Oh, You'd love me no matter what I did!" And I got up leaving His loving presence because I didn't "feel" that I deserved it. After inquiring of my pastor later that afternoon, I realized I *had* believed a false accusation. I had not *divided asunder* my *soul* and *spirit* which is a necessary ingredient to rest (Heb. 4:12). I was led by my "feeler" and not by my "knower" and had rejected the affections of my Beloved for no reason that morning. True rest comes as the bride seeks to know the Groom *by the spirit.* The soul must be kept out of the leadership role so the lies of the Accuser cannot intrude upon us. And our soul must be renewed by the Word of God to agree with our spirit (Rom. 12:2). We must lay our soul (self-life) down, i.e., submit it to our reborn spirit in order to enter His rest.

Next I learned that there is also a **rest while in temptation.** The Tempter attacked me with sinful thoughts. (He puts them in your mind and then accuses you of having them there.) My being, overly-busy at the time, delayed my response, and the thoughts had escalated in frequency and torment. They were sinful and I loathed them. Again, the Lord would manifest His love toward me. I would say, "Lord, how can You love me with these thoughts in my mind?" He'd reply, "They are not yours," and would also continue to express His love for me. That blew me away. Was He accepting me? Yes. But not the thoughts, because tempting thoughts can easily take on flesh and evolve into sinful actions. I knew I could not play with this temptation. I knew this was a serious threat. Yet I tried to repent, resist, rebuke, and cast out, only to achieve short-lived victory time and time again. I was totally impotent in my own deliverance. As I began to earnestly seek the Lord, He brought me the answer.

God promised to fight our battles (Gen. 15:1). In the dismal days when multiple enemies surrounded Jerusalem while King Jehoshaphat reigned, he sought God, trusting in that very promise. The Spirit of God answered confirming this promise through a Levite singer named Jahaziel. He prophesied, "The battle is not yours, but God's . . . Ye shall not need to fight in this battle: set yourselves, stand ye still, and see the salvation of the Lord with you" (2 Chron. 20:15b, 17). The word "set" means "to take a position": "to stand still," meaning "to stop," or "leave off." The people of Judah left off relying on their own military might and *rested* in Jehovah's supernatural might and intervention. They rested in Jehovah, and He destroyed their enemies *for* them. Totally frustrated in my own powerlessness, and at my wit's end, I readily handed my battle over to the Lord. That was what He had been waiting for. He swiftly took the lead, and immediately, I was free. What a rest we have in Jesus!

Rest is wonderful. It is a by-product of being radically in love with Jesus, utterly abandoned to Him. I know you are already wondering, *How do I do that? How do I fall in love with Jesus again?* Actually, it is rest and not work that rekindles our first love for Jesus. Not *doing* but *being*. Did you have to *work* at falling in love with your spouse? Try plan A, then plan B? No. Just the touch of his hand, the smile on her face, and the sparkle of his eyes melted your heart. You just found yourself in love. You didn't *climb* up to love; you *fell* in love. No effort. No strategy. No work. You didn't even arrange it. You hoped for it, but it wasn't intentional. It just happened. It is the same with Jesus. Rest. Read His love letters. Spend time with Him. Just *be* with Him.

Imagine a husband sitting in his easy chair at the end of his workday while his wife is picking up papers, sorting clothes, and polishing the furniture. He sits there longing for her just to sit down beside him, but she's crisscrossing the room with meticulous busyness. He longs for fellowship with her, but she is preoccupied with work. Finally, he says, "Honey, please just sit down. I just want to *be* with you. I just want to talk with you. You don't have to do anything to please me. I just want *you*." That is what Jesus is saying to us. Come. Set aside your activities. Stop *doing*. *Be* with Him. He loves you. Remember when you dated your honey? Every time you met you weren't excited about the movie you would see or the menu at the restaurant. You just wanted to *be* together. What you *did* together was irrelevant. That is a portrait of His love and rest for us.

Who initiates a marital union? The groom, of course. Jesus, through the Holy Spirit, is ever coming to woo and court His bride. And all you have to do to get His attention is breathe. He is already madly in love with you. He has had His eyes on you since the foundation of time; you are a captivating delight to Him. You don't have to *do* anything to get His attention, love, or favor. You already have His undivided attention, His tender love and complete devotion. The cross proved that. You could never *do* enough to earn it. But then it's free! Jesus is the head of this union, and life in oneness with Christ is like dancing a waltz. We merely enjoy the embrace of His arms of love and gaze into His eyes as He leads us gracefully about the dance floor of life flowing in true harmony of spirit and soul. We move as one. It is not work. **Our romance with the Lord is *rest*!** Enjoy Him! Enjoy your time together! Keep casting all your care on Him for, He cares for you. Enter His rest.

CHAPTER 5

WATCH OF THE BRIDE

And thou shalt observe the feast of weeks . . . (Exod. 34:22a)

Our keeping the Feast of Unleavened Bread and Sabbath, by *cleaving to Christ and resting in Him*, are often empowered and sustained by regularly keeping the Feast of Weeks, or Pentecost. It is called the Feast of Weeks because there were seven weeks and one day between the Passover and Pentecost. Forty-nine plus one is fifty, and fifty is the number for Jubilee or liberty. Liberty comes with this feast! Remember the original *Pentecost* was staged at Mt Sinai. It was the marriage covenant cut by Jehovah God with Israel. The new marriage covenant promised by Jesus at Passover was cut on the cross. Forty days after His resurrection from the grave, Jesus prepared His disciples for the promised outpouring of the Spirit (Acts 1:4), commanding them to wait together. They mutually obeyed for ten days nonstop. Right on the feast day of Pentecost, when multitudes flocked to Jerusalem, God's fire fell (Acts 2:1-4), and the newborn church was ignited with power to reach the lost. Yet this great start was described prophetically as merely "the former rain in moderation" by the prophet Joel (Joel 2:23a). That day did not fully complete Pentecost.

There is yet a finalization of Pentecost for and through the church. It will be a far, far greater outpouring of God's Spirit for it was defined as "the former" and heavier "latter rain" together (Joel 2:23b). Like the original 120 believers in the upper room, we must purposely and expectantly tarry and wait together for this greater outpouring of His Spirit. It is God's chosen design for our accelerated maturation and purification as the end-day bride that we may reap a boundless harvest of souls in the closing days!

This greater Pentecost looms on our immediate horizon. God calls the end-day church to keep Pentecost in multiple levels: globally, collectively, and individually. Globally, the church is called to gather together on Pentecost and seek His face for this greater outpouring of His Spirit. In the 1990s it was internationally recognized as Jesus Day. It is currently called the Global Day of Prayer (GDOP).[13] Yet there is more we can personally or collectively do on a continual basis for our preparation.

As a nation, traditional Jews celebrate Pentecost or *Shavuot* annually with an all-night watch. We too are called to do so, but not just annually. We are to keep it individually and collectively through a watchful lifestyle. But one wonderful way to maintain our personal Pentecost is to keep what is called the Watch of the Bride enmeshed with the Sabbath rest each week. As we approach the close of this age, the bridal watch should evolve into continual 24/7/365 ministry of prayer and praise scripturally referred to as rebuilding the Tabernacle of David (Amos 9:11; Acts 15:16-17) to reach the masses of lost souls. The expectant bride, like the five wise virgins, willingly awaits and thereby prepares for the return of her Groom. And the fruit of keeping this feast is incredibly delightful! It produces revelatory intima-

[13] www.gdopusa.com

cy and renewal. The revelatory intimacy is our knowing Christ and being known of Him as well as prophetic insights into our present time, season, and destiny. The renewal encompasses spiritual "times of refreshing" (Acts 3:19), the restoration of our soul, good physical health (Jer. 8:22), deliverance, joy, and prosperity. Within Pentecost we are being transformed from glory to glory into His very image! Of course, I didn't know any of this until a particular encounter with God.

Eleven intercessors and I visited the Toronto Airport Christian Fellowship (TACF) renewal services in Toronto, Ontario, Canada, in late 1995, where I was radically touched by the Lord. In fact, I was literally tossed around like a rag doll. Refreshed and revived, I drove the van-load of ladies home on Saturday, October 28, 1995. During the drive, three times I saw myself lying on three front chairs in our sanctuary all night. It seemed odd to me. I had never heard of such a thing. When we arrived, it was late at night, and our pastor was praying in the sanctuary. I didn't want to disturb him and have him question my impression. I prayed briefly in the hallway to allay the burden and salve my conscience and then drove home. As soon as I arrived, the Lord directed me, in very firm intonations, to read Joel chapter one. I read it trembling on my knees. When I read "priests . . . come lie all night" (Joel 1:13), I knew I had *royally* missed it.

The next day, the Sunday morning service was dry as a sun-bleached bone. The evening service was even drier, but what really disturbed me was that two missionaries and my pastor were sitting on the exact three chairs upon which the Lord had impressed me to lie. Then He whispered to my heart that He had wanted to bless them but could not because I had not *interceded* for them. Who would think that lying down all night would be intercession? But it is. That began my Holy Ghost tutorial on the watch nights. There are four watches of the Greek or Roman night: "at even, or at midnight, at the cockcrowing, or in the morning" (Mark 13:34). In modern terms they are designated as 6 p.m. to 9 p.m., 9 p.m. to midnight, midnight to 3 a.m., and 3 a.m. to 6 a.m. Jesus kept these watches. Sometimes, He rose early in the morning in the fourth watch. Often, He stayed up late for the second and even third watch. One time, after ministering to the multitudes, Jesus went up in the hills to pray into the fourth watch and then walked upon wind-tossed waves to succor His distraught disciples (Matt. 14:22-27) aboard a ship struggling in the tempest. Our Groom prayerfully kept *all* the watches the night before He selected His twelve disciples (Luke 6:12-13). He led us by example to keep these watches too.

After my failing, I pleaded with the Lord for another watch. He graciously gave me one. I knew that I was to be at the sanctuary by 10 p.m. that Saturday night and to lie down on the platform behind the podium at midnight, remaining there until 6 a.m. Sunday morning. From ten to twelve midnight, I prayed and sang to Him, walking and dancing about the sanctuary. Then I laid down behind the podium at midnight. Instantly I knew that I was lying on the threshing floor at the feet of my Kinsman Redeemer, just as Ruth had done at the feet of Boaz. I felt Him spread His skirt over me. I was delighted to be with Him; His presence was very tangible. As the hours slipped away, I wondered when I would sleep. Finally I asked Him. He replied, "It says 'lie all night,' not sleep all night." "Oh," I said. It was all so new to me. Around 5:45 a.m., He told me to get up and go home. I started to argue with Him that it was not 6:00 a.m., but He insisted. As I left, I noticed the predawn darkness. Forms and figures could barely be discerned. I hurried home and prepared for worship service. I couldn't wait to return home after the service to read the book of Ruth, where I discovered a goldmine of revelation on night watches.

Widowed Naomi heard that "the Lord had visited his people in giving them bread" (1:6). (Remember, in spiritual terms, *bread* refers to "revelation.") She and her daughter-in-law, Ruth, also a widow, together returned to Bethlehem, which means "house of bread," at the beginning of the barley harvest. (Barley is the primary grain of the first or early harvest season, and it is known for its special renewing nutrients. After a long winter without fresh food, barley renewed physical health and strength.) This whole story of Ruth spans the fifty days of the early harvest between Passover and Pentecost. (For us it means the span of time from our Lord's death, burial, and resurrection until the greater outpouring of His Spirit soon to come.)

Ruth, as a type of the bride being made ready, received great grace and favor with the owner of the fields. For several days, she gleaned in the fields as they were harvested. As the harvest season neared its end before Pentecost, Ruth (as instructed by Naomi) went to *lie* on the threshing floor at the feet of her kinsman redeemer, Boaz, "all night" (3:7). He awoke at *midnight* and Ruth asked Boaz to spread his skirt over her (3:8, 9). She was asking him to marry her. He agreed to pursue her request. He told her to "tarry for the night" (3:13), or keep the full night watch. In the morning "she rose up before one could know another" (3:14) just as I had. Boaz would not let her go away empty but blessed her with six measures of barley from the harvest (3:15-17). Later, the redemption he bought included the redemption of Naomi's land.

As we lay in the watch night at the feet of our Kinsman Redeemer, Jesus, the wind of His Spirit is removing the chaff from our souls (as on a threshing floor) so that we become a spotless bride. His skirt spread over us speaks of protection, the marital protection of the husband for his wife. And as we seek intimacy of the Bridegroom, the blessings of redemption become ours including the redemption of *our* land: our home, our street, our community, and our city, for they are the ones over which we are watching. And He will see that we *too* receive our portion of blessing, i.e., renewal, revelation, health, prosperity, and a harvest of souls! Upon this revelation, my willingness to keep the night watches increased immensely, and it even became easier with time. In fact, it became wonderful! I couldn't wait for Him to give me a watch. You see, when experiencing personal Pentecost, the watches are no longer a duty. A bride is so in love with her groom that she doesn't care about sleep. He will tug at her heartstrings to draw her away with Him into the secret place, His chamber of love. Somehow, no sleep becomes refreshing. It doesn't make sense in the natural, but then it *is super*natural, but only as He leads.

I quickly learned that when I kept a watch on my own initiative, it was hard and tiring with no fruit. But if I waited and received one from the Lord, His grace would enable me to carry it out, and the results were incredible! The watches I kept alone were usually on Saturday nights, and they varied from week to week, much like our Lord's did. Sometimes, I watched for a single three-hour watch, sometimes two, sometimes three. Sometimes, tearful intercession and travail erupted in the midst of it. Sometimes, quiet and peace prevailed. Sometimes, dancing in pure joy and holy laughter took me for a spin. It was, and is, glorious! And I learned that there are rewards for keeping the watches. When I obediently watched, the next day, during the Sunday morning or evening services, my Lord would point out to me the person for whom I had interceded. When I didn't, He would point out the one who was not blessed or healed or delivered as a consequence of my disobedience. I distinctly remember one Sunday evening as He showed me the teenage girl that He had desired to deliver through my intercession. But I had not totally obeyed. I was called over by a ministry leader to assist in her deliverance. But, in actuality, I was called over by God to look into the eyes of the one I had failed. Thank God He quickly forgives when we repent! By then I was addicted to continuing.

After a couple of years of this grand personal adventure, the Lord spoke to a group of eight intercessors (seven others and me) to *keep* the watch *together* each week on Friday nights as a collective Sabbath rest. (The Hebrew Sabbath starts Friday at sundown and continues to Saturday at sundown.) Prophetically, the Lord told us that each one of us was watching over five hundred souls as we lay in His presence. The meaning of the word "watch" includes "protection as by a guard." We were each guarding over the lives of 500 people (saints or lost ones) in the weekly Watch of the Bride. Shortly thereafter, during an informal Saturday night gathering to praise the Lord, several members shared how they had been protected from accidents or suddenly healed. Our eyes connected with each other. We secretly knew that God was showing us the results of our intercession.

Our little band of extravagant worshippers named our watch night *Date Night with the Jesus!* Together, we earnestly looked forward to it every week. Once the clock struck 10 p.m. Friday night, we agreed to fellowship only with the Father, the Son, and the Holy Spirit and not with each other until 6 a.m. Saturday morning. Praise and worship, spontaneous dancing or intercession, prophetic actions, new songs, and just lying in His radiant presence described the night's impromptu format. A passionate exchange of love described its mood. Each lady's life reflected the renewing process and return to her first love. There is such joy in His presence! And that joy is our strength!

Is this just for intercessors? No. Jesus commanded His disciples of *all* ages to *watch* and pray (Matt. 24:42; Mark 13:33).

On March 26, 1999 (almost four years from the start of keeping the night watches), approximately one hundred members of our local body collectively kept the Friday night watch from 10 p.m. until 2 a.m. According to Isaiah 40:31, as we collectively wait upon Him, He has promised to renew our strength that we mount up with wings as eagles, we run and not be weary, and we walk and not faint. That is corporate renewal! It is seeking of God's face *together*, as did the Israelites at the original Pentecost at Mt. Sinai and the 120 in the upper room. That night the anointing was heavy on the youth band as they played continually all four hours. Instead of eight ladies watching over four thousand souls, approximately one hundred members were guarding over fifty thousand souls!

The Lord spoke a word to my heart that night referring to Paul Yonggi Cho's church, which kept the Friday watch night from its conception. He said, "The souls they diligently and faithfully watched over became the largest church in the earth today!" Around 1 a.m. wails, howls, cries, and weeping began to sound throughout the sanctuary as God touched the hearts of Spirit-inebriated saints, propelling them into deep intercession. That following Sunday, March 28, there was a refreshing move of God's Spirit in the morning service. Many souls were touched and released. The impact of the watchful bride is awesome! Imagine the impact of multiple congregations keeping the Watch of the Bride together or in turn. Then imagine the impact of a 24/7/365 watch called the Tabernacle of David along with the annual collective gathering now called the Global Day of Prayer on Pentecost Sunday. Whole communities can be taken from darkness into the light of Christ.

What does a watch night look like? In any watch night, we always want to center on our Lord. Jesus is the reason. Jesus is the theme. The five wise virgins tarried for the Groom, not each other! It is a time to focus our fellowship with Him and not each other. Music (live or recorded) sets a wonderful atmosphere inducing praise, worship, and intimate fellowship. Whether you are singing or speaking words of adoration to Him, do it with all your heart. As you seek Him, He will *touch* you by His Spirit. He may spontaneously thrust you into dance, new songs, warfare, prophetic proclamations, or intercession and travail to release the transforming Life and power of God. Feel free to wave praise banners or lie and pray under a prayer banner. But most importantly, as His weighty glory comes upon you, sit or lie down and soak in His presence. Some may choose to organize the night with formal times of praise, prayer, and proclamation. But others may just let it happen. It is best however the Lord leads.

What is going on in the watch to prepare us as His bride? We are prepared by the Holy Spirit coming to us to . . .

1. **Soak us**
2. **Sit on us**
3. **Reveal His Person to us**
4. **Bring us revelation**
5. **Heal and transform us**

1. First and foremost, He soaks us to prepare us for the new wine, i.e., His manifest presence is wherever we go. It is like the stomach of a goat the ancient Israelites used as a suitable wineskin. It was suitable because it was very flexible. As the new wine fermented, the skin could swell with the fermenting process without tear or rupture. With time, however, a wineskin could gradually dry out and lose its suitable suppleness and eventually become rigid. Jesus confirmed that new wine could not be put into old bottles (Matt. 9:15-17). Dried and unyielding, the old skins would break and be destroyed, and the new wine would be lost. But should old wineskins be soaked in water or oil, their flexibility would be restored. We are each a wineskin. We may have been hardened (become negative, critical, religious, judgmental, etc.). God wants us pliable for the new move of His Spirit, the new wine, to contain it and flow with it, for He has saved the best *wine* for last (John 2:10)!

Rain is a wonderful symbol of *soaking*, as found in the book of Joel. A soaking rain reverses and remedies the numerous dry conditions of the church of which Joel addressed in natural terms (1:1-2:11). Spiritual rain softens hard, dry hearts just as natural rain does hardened soil. It causes withered fruits (1:12), the fruit of the Spirit, to abound (2:22). It makes the perishing crops (1:12, 17) to flourish (2:24) so there is meal for the bread of revelation. This rain replenishes the dried up rivers (1:20) and the supply of oil from the olive trees (1:10) as the anointing and the gifts of the Spirit flow freely once again (2:24). The advancing armies (2:1-11) of judgment and discipline (Lev. 26 and Deut. 28) are driven back (2:20, 25). Losses and other resulting consequences of years of disobedience (1:4) are quickly reversed (2:25). The regenerative power of His rain brings deadened people and ministries to Life. It is a *soaking* that we desperately need, and it is refreshing to our soul! By it, we take on His character. Like a dry sponge plunged into water, we become like the One who saturates our soul. Whether in a night watch or not, *soaking* in His presence is vital to our maturation and transformation.

2. The Holy Spirit also comes to sit upon us just as He sat on the early believers in Acts 2:3 to kick-start the newborn church. But now He comes to mature and purify the end-day church as prophesied by the prophet Malachi.

> **Behold, I *will* send my messenger, and he shall prepare the way before me: and the LORD, whom ye seek, shall suddenly come to his temple, even the messenger of the covenant, whom ye delight in: behold, he *shall* come, saith the LORD of hosts. But who *may* abide the day of his coming? and who *shall* stand when he appeareth? for he *is* like a refiner's fire, and like fullers' soap: And he shall sit as a refiner and purifier of silver: and he shall purify the sons of Levi, and purge them as gold and silver, that they may offer unto the LORD an offering in righteousness...And I will come near to you to judgment . . . (MAL. 3:1-3, 5a)**

The Holy Spirit comes as the Refiner's fire to sit on us, His living temples and priests[14] (sons of Levi), to purify us in character (gold) for miraculous ministry (silver). Judgment begins with the house of God (1 Pet. 4:17) and concludes with "the day of vengeance of our God" upon the world (Isaiah 61:2b) and those who would not leave it. Don't wait until *that day* to seek God. Seek Him *now*. Be purified and made ready *now*.

The Refiner's fire purifies us much like the goldsmith does gold. The goldsmith heats up the gold until it is molten. This causes the impurities to rise to the surface. Then he skims off the impurities and takes a full-faced look into the liquid gold. If his reflection is not clear, he will heat the gold even more until all the impurities are removed and he clearly sees his reflection in the gold. Gold scripturally refers to divine character. Our character must be as His for His glory. We must display *His character.* Godly character (gold) flows best with empowered ministry (silver). When we reflect His character, that is, His love nature, then He will permit the *acts of Christ* or glory to manifest through us in power as embodied by the Feast of

[14] Jesus Christ "hath made us kings and priests unto God His Father" (Rev. 1:9)

Tabernacles.

In the night watches, our refinement is accelerated. As the Holy Refining Spirit sits on us, He will convince us of any sin lurking within our soul. He will bring it to the surface and then lead us to repentance. Andrew Murray poignantly declared that the depth of our repentance will determine the extent of our revival, personally and collectively. Permit Him time and opportunity to sit on you. And remember, it is hard to sit on something that is in constant motion. He said, "Be still, and know that I am God" (Ps. 46:10a). As He broods and hovers over you, let Him confront your hidden sins, wrong motives, and bad attitudes. Don't make excuses for them. Be purified! This is the working out of the salvation of our souls toward maturity in Christ. As with Jacob, He may not just sit but *wrestle* with our self-life, pride, and rebellion through the night until we, like Jacob, stop our striving in the flesh and limp or lean on Christ in us. Only then can He bless us with a new name as Revelation 2:17 promises just as Jacob (deceiver) became Israel (prince of God). Bad attitudes, fears, anger, and deep emotional wounds will heal and vanish without scar or evidence that they were ever within us. It is a marvel, something we could never do ourselves.

Sometimes the work is so deep that we may fall naturally asleep or enter a deep, probing, supernatural sleep. The Father put Adam into a deep sleep while He fashioned Eve. Within the depths of His presence, the Father, by His Spirit, is forming within us the appropriate character of the bride so that He may present us to His Son, the last Adam, a "glorious bride not having spot, or wrinkle, or any such thing" (Eph. 5:27). Jehovah also put Abram into a deep sleep in Genesis 15:9-17 as He cut covenant with him. Our lying, even sleeping, at our Lord's feet is a time in which our soul is discerned and divided asunder from our spirit that we might lay down our self-life to receive His abundant life. And as a *deep sleep* comes upon us, He whispers and reveals to our hearts the promises of our marriage covenant with Christ and reveals to us things to come just as He did with Abraham.

3. As we keep the watches, we develop a deeper intimate knowledge of the Lord. There is an old secular song whose lyrics I tweaked a bit from a bridal perspective. They aptly describe the outcome of this feast: "Getting to know You, getting to know all about You; getting to love You, getting to know You love me.[15]" Like Moses, such was the cry of the apostle Paul's bridal heart.

> **[For my determined purpose is] that I may know** {ginosko} **Him [that I may progressively become more deeply and intimately acquainted with Him, perceiving and recognizing and understanding the wonders of His Person more strongly and more clearly], and that I may in that same way come to know the power outflowing from His resurrection [which it exerts over believers], and that I may so share His sufferings as to be continually transformed [in spirit into His likeness even] to His death, [in the hope] That if possible I may attain to the [spiritual and moral] resurrection [that lifts me] out from among the dead [even while in the body]. (PHIL. 3:10-11, AMP; BRACKETS IN THE ORIGINAL)**

"That I may know him" is the cry of the bride. There are two Greek words translated "know" in the New Testament Scriptures. They are *oida* and *ginosko*. Oida means "you know that

[15] Oscar Hammerstein II and Richard Rogers, "Getting to Know You," the *King and I: A Decca Broadway Original Cast Album,* Decca, 1951, 33 1/3 rpm. The actual lyrics are "Getting to know you, getting to know all about you. Getting to like you, getting to hope you like me."

you know." For example, once saved, you know that your name is written in the Lamb's book of Life even though you have never seen it. You just know (oida) it! It is by the spirit. It is a perfect knowledge. This "know" also refers to words of knowledge and other revelatory gifts. Ginosko, on the other hand, means "to progressively come to know." It requires time and effort, for it involves the soul (mind, will, and emotions). As a husband and wife grow, mature, and experience life together over the years, they increasingly learn of each other's tastes, attitudes, strengths, and weaknesses. The discoveries never end. And as long as they pursue their marital commitment one with another, they will continue to know (ginosko) each other more and more. This is the "know" which Paul desired.

Jesus knew (oida) His Father. They were in perfect union. In John 17:22 He said, "we are one." His earnest desire is that we also be one in them. His union with the Father always was and is in the realm of the spirit, for in John 7:29 Jesus said of the Father, "I know [oida] him: for I am from him and he hath sent me." The Son of God knew and was known of His Father by the Spirit for all eternity. They fellowshipped Spirit to Spirit before time existed, and they will continue to do so forever. And yet Jesus also used ginosko to describe His fellowship with His Father from His new prospective as a spirit (*pneuma*) and soul (*pseuche*) encased within a flesh body on a natural planet amidst sin, death, and darkness (John 10:15). There were areas of His soul impacted by humanity that He and His Father had to *get to know*. So it is with our fellowship with Jesus (John 10:14). It begins in the spirit as we are born again. It is perfect and complete in the spirit, but our fellowship must grow with mutual attentiveness of our soul as well. That requires time and effort. An individual daily watch before work in the early morning hours or late at night when the household is quiet is excellent for our personal fellowship. But a collective Friday watch night or any regular watch night is also a perfect time for unfolding intimate fellowship *together* through extensive exposure to His presence.

By the way, Paul was not content with just knowing Christ. He longed for Christ to know him, that is, to be known of Him. After Paul professes, "That I may know him" in verse 10, Paul continues in verse 12 with, "I follow after, if that I may apprehend that for which also I am apprehended of Christ Jesus." In other words, he desired to be known of the One he was pursuing to know. The lyrics of another renewal song (based on this passage) clarify his heart's cry: "It is You, it is You, it is You that I love. It is You my Lord and King, I apprehend to know and be known.[16]" That is a portion of our personal Pentecost. The bride purposes to know Him by taking the necessary time in the night watches to be with Him, listening, waiting, enjoying His presence, and pondering His words. The bride's *responding* and *submitting* to His Love-generated leadings, dealings, and even His crushings (as He sits on us) permits us to be known by Him.

> **But if one loves God truly [with affectionate reverence, prompt obedience, and grateful recognition of His blessing], he is known by God [recognized as worthy of His intimacy and love, and he is owned by Him]. (1 Cor. 8:3, AMP; brackets in the original)**

We were bought with the blood of the Lamb. We are His. But true intimacy must penetrate and conquer every dimension of our triune being. Every crack and crevice must open up to the light of His glory. The hidden dark depths of emotional despair, stubbornness of will, analytical thinking, temptations, fears—whatever is there—must be shared with Him and submitted to

[16] Pete Sanchez Jr., "It Is You," *I Exalt Thee*, CD Track 15, Integrity's Hosanna! Music, Capitol CMG Publishing (IMI), 1983.

Him. True lasting relationships are based on transparency and truth to ourselves and especially to our Lord. This mutually expanding love builds upon our union of spirit. For (agape) love "is the bond of perfectness" (Col. 3:14), meaning the perfect uniting principle of soul to soul.

4. With the watch comes what the prophet Joel calls *the meal* from which they made bread. This "meal" means "grain." Bread is made from grain but this bread also refers to revelation and prophetic insight.

> **And it shall come to pass afterward, that I will pour out my spirit upon all flesh; and your sons and your daughters shall prophesy, your old men shall dream dreams, your young men shall see visions: (Joel 2:28)**

It was in the depths of sleep that angels brought messages; end-time prophecies were revealed (Dan. 8:18-26); and Messiah appeared (Dan. 10:4-8). And even now, the secrets of God, dreams, and visions are ever increasing in magnitude and profundity across the earth. Many of these wonderful encounters with God come in natural sleep or within the supernatural *deep sleep* of His glorious presence. Our personal or collective watches of the night are the perfect environment for His bestowing visions and dreams and revelation, understanding His Word, gaining insights into our destinies, and receiving instructions for obedient lives. And it seems that revelation particularly comes forth in the fourth watch.

5. In addition to emotional restoration and character transformation, physical healing also comes in the watches. During my yearly gynecological checkup in 1997, my doctor discovered a lump under my left arm. With a mother and two aunts having already experienced breast cancer, she advised me to schedule a sonogram. I had already been impressed to fast and pray in our sanctuary during the Ten Days of Awe preceding the Feast of Tabernacles that year. It was a week away, so I purposely scheduled the sonogram *after* my ten day rendezvous. What a wonderful ten days I had with the Lord, singing and soaking, praising and dancing, listening and hearing. Then I went for my sonogram. The technician scanned under my arm repeatedly. I could tell he was frustrated. He brought in a doctor and they searched. Finally, he admitted that he could not detect anything. Just then, I heard the title of Rich Cook's song: "Jesus Your Presence Makes Me Whole." In His presence we are healed. The Bible declares this.

> **Is there no balm in Gilead? Is there no physician there? Why then is not the health of the daughter of my people restored? [Because Zion no longer enjoyed the presence of the Great Physician!] (Jer. 8:22)**

God is asking, "Why are My people not healthy?" And then He answers His own question. "They are not spending time in My presence." The Lord, our Healer and Great Physician, stands ready to apply His healing balm to us as we tarry and wait upon Him in the watches of the night or day.

Through the watches we are personally being prepared for our Lord's return. But our watching will also benefit others. Our union with Christ brings forth spiritual conception, birth, and *children*! Right now there are *multitudes* in the valley of decision. Masses of people in darkness are about to be violently snatched from the clutches of Satan's twisted and warped talons and graciously thrust into our Father's everlasting arms of love. Daniel prophesied in Daniel 11:32, "The people that do know their God shall be strong, and do exploits" in these last days. Twice, in the Song of Solomon, the bride is described as "terrible as an army with banners" (6:4, 6:10). The end-day bride will be a warring bride, warring and travailing for the souls of men. These are the children to fill the Father's house, for He commanded us, "Be fruitful and multiply" (Gen. 1:28). The bride's ability to draw lost souls to Christ comes from her union with Christ. She becomes like Him. They are one in character and in miraculous ministry. Purity and power go hand in hand. The lost will be readily convinced when *both* His nature *and* His works are displayed by His winsome bride made ready. The awakened church keeping Pentecost will display His manifest presence, which is our Feast of Tabernacles!

There is also reemerging a continual watch before our Lord's return that *commands* the harvest. It is not a weekly watch or just the 24/7 watches of the Ten Days of Prayer preceding the present Global Day of Prayer on Pentecost Sunday.[17] Anna "served God with fasting and prayers night and day" and she saw her prayers answered in the *first* coming of Messiah (Luke 2:36-38). Can any less be required for His second coming? A 24/7/365 prayer movement is rising in the earth preparing the way for our Lord's return and the coming massive harvest of souls. It parallels the strategy of the ancient farmers. They set up watchtowers all over their fields. Right before and during the harvest season, they manned the towers twenty-four hours a day to ensure the harvest was not stolen or destroyed by their enemies. Jesus spoke to every generation of Christians when He said, "Lift up your eyes, and look on the fields; for they are white [or ripe] already to harvest" (John 4:35). Whole cities will be taken in these last days, if the bride made ready keeps these watches regularly and collectively around the clock, rebuilding what is called the Tabernacle of David (Amos 9:11, Acts 15:16-17). It is a continual Watch of the Bride and its time is now! Let's keep the feasts the New Covenant way!

[17] Global Day of Prayer 2005-2014 and thereafter.

CHAPTER 6

PREPARING FOR TRANSFORMATION

Just prior to the Feast of Tabernacles, there is a special **forty-day season called *Teshuvah*.** It originated with the second forty days Moses spent on Mt. Sinai in deep repentance for Israel's sin with the calf, beginning on *Rosh Chodesh* and ending on the Day of Atonement. Forty days was the required preparatory period of time necessary to receive such extensive Torah (or bridal revelation). This Torah included the second two tablets of testimony, and volumes of instruction for all of Israel, and also a personal revelation of Jehovah to Moses (as a bride being made ready), found in the text of Exodus chapter 34.

> **And the LORD passed by before him, and proclaimed, The LORD, The LORD God, merciful and gracious, longsuffering, and abundant in goodness and truth, Keeping mercy for thousands, forgiving iniquity and transgression and sin, and *that* will by no means clear *the guilty*; visiting the iniquity of the fathers upon the children, and upon the children's children, unto the third and to the fourth *generation*. And Moses made haste, and bowed his head toward the earth, and worshipped. (Exod. 34:6-8)**

This very passage, called the Thirteen Attributes of God, is recited daily by practicing Jews during this forty-day season. Forty is the number of testing, cleansing, and purification: testing (as in the two forty-day periods of Moses on Mount Sinai and the forty days of Jesus in the wilderness) and cleansing and purification (as in the forty days of rain in Noah's flood and the forty measures of water in the ritual purification bath). For the Jews, these forty days are a period of intense introspection and repentance for the purpose of coming closer to God and recognizing one's life purpose or destiny. So is it also for the bride of Christ. For forty days the Jews of Israel go to pray at the Western Wall in Jerusalem, but we are to go to the wall of intense self-examination in Christ.

The **first thirty days of *Teshuvah*** encompasses the entire sixth month of the Hebrew religious calendar, Elul.[18] The word "Elul" comes from the four Hebrew letters (aleph—lamed—vav—lamed), which are the first four letters of Song of Solomon 6:3: "I am my beloved's and my beloved is mine." Thirty is the number of consecration, with definite bridal implication from this Song of Solomon passage. According to 1 Pet. 2:9, all Christians are consecrated in spirit by our Lord unto our Lord as a "holy nation" and "royal priesthood" to serve and worship Him in spirit and in truth (Jn. 4:24). But our full consecration encompasses more. It includes the total devotion and dedication of our soul toward Him, much like a love-sick bride toward her beloved groom. Our consecration must be of spirit *and* soul. Jesus made the way (Heb. 10:20) by His blood to this place of priestly status and ministry before the very throne of God, but we have a choice. We may squander this priceless position and

[18] Elul is the twelfth month of the Jewish civil year and the sixth month of the ecclesiastical (religious) year on the Hebrew calendar. It is a summer month of twenty-nine days. Yet it is considered thirty days here because it starts on the eve of the last day of the fifth month. It is written both as "Elul" or "Ellul."

wander through our Christian lifetime around the perimeter of the courtyard, or we may embrace this consecration bestowed upon us and press in to enter beyond the veil into the glory realm of our magnificent King on a regular basis. Though the privilege and place is ours, it is often our own misplaced priorities that detour us from living in His face. Without true meticulous self-introspection, only eruptions of divine judgment will startle and awaken us to realize our vacated position in Christ, vacated by our lapsed devotion to Him. There are two stories recorded in Old Testament Scripture during the first of Elul which illustrate to us two historical responses. One response we must avoid; one we should follow.

Around 600 to 622 BCE, before Judah's captivity in Babylon in 597 BCE, Ezekiel wrote of the first incident. Starting in chapter 8, we find Ezekiel (like the remnant bride in preparation) at home on the fifth day, "the number of grace," of the sixth month, Elul, when the hand of the Lord came mightily upon him. He received a revelation of the glory of the Lord. He saw the Lord with fire from His waist down and a brilliant radiance from His waist upward. The Spirit of God then took Ezekiel to the north gate of the temple in Jerusalem. There, He grievously showed Ezekiel the "seat of the image jealousy, which provoketh to jealousy" (Ezek. 8:3b). It was a false Babylonian deity called Tammuz, or Dumuzi. Jehovah then showed Ezekiel the seventy ancients, the Sanhedrin, doing abominations with idols right on the temple grounds; some women weeping over Tammuz; and twenty-five men worshipping the sun. Misplaced devotion had spread throughout both the *clergy* and *laity* of the church of Judah. Though consecrated as a nation to Jehovah, their passion was observably for others. In a grand finale response to their continued adultery, God's Sh'khinah glory lifted out from the Holy of Holies. Six angels then appeared and marked the heads of all the people who hated these abominations, the remnant bride. Swiftly, judgment was set in order for the destruction of those unmarked. It was a point in time when God said something like, "Enough! You haven't judged yourselves, so I will judge you." Those who were not devoted unto Him would soon be slaughtered by the Babylonians.

Jehovah's glory then departed from the East Gate of the temple toward the Mount of Olives and ascended to heaven leaving the temple Icabod. His manifest presence was gone, for the majority of Judah had neglected her marriage vows as Zephaniah so poignantly wrote.

> **She obeyed not the voice; she received not correction; she trusted not in the LORD; she drew not near to her God. (Zeph. 3:2)**

And yet even God's judgment was and still is a work of His grace! Should He have done nothing, they would have never recognized their deadly condition. Because Judah did *not* judge themselves, they forced God to send (meaning "permit") judgments upon them to shake them to spiritual sobriety. Had even the remnant bride of that time risen from her complacency and ardently interceded for the straying majority as did Moses, many would not have perished or been taken captive by Babylon. We are no different today. The glory has departed from most of the church due to our general deficiency of devotion. The bride being made ready must intercede that the body of Christ does not drift away from their faith.

The second account was recorded in the book of Haggai, and it turns out much better. It occurred after Israel returned from Babylonian captivity around 557 to 525 BCE. They *had learned* from their previous waywardness. On the first day of the month of Elul (1 Elul), God sent the prophet Haggai to Zerubabel, the governor of Jerusalem, and to Joshua the High Priest (Hag. 1:3-

8). Jehovah confronted them with a disturbing truth. The people were living in beautifully finished houses, but God's house was a neglected waste. He warned them to consider their ways, i.e., search their own hearts, for their priorities were awry. Yahweh was saying, "*My* house is a waste. Is My beloved, the one I set apart for Me, concerned with *My* house?" Are *we* truly concerned with His priorities? That is a question we all must ask ourselves.

Jehovah then verbally captured their attention with their pressing circumstances, which were His permitted judgments described in everyday terms. "Ye have sown much, and bring in little; ye eat, but ye have not enough; ye drink, but ye are not filled with drink; ye clothe you, but there is none warm; and he that earneth wages earneth wages to put it into a bag with holes" (Hag. 1:6). Sound familiar? The blessings had ceased. They never had enough. They were never fully satisfied. They were dry. They were in need. Again, Jehovah warned them to consider their ways or priorities, and then He added this glorious promise should they obey:

> **Go up to the hill country and bring lumber and rebuild [My] house, and I will take pleasure in it and I will be glorified, says the Lord [by accepting it as done for My glory and by displaying My glory in it]. (HAG. 1:8, AMP; BRACKETS IN THE ORIGINAL)**

He promised them that if they would judge their own hearts, repent, and consecrate themselves wholly to Him, pursuing His priorities (namely the temple at that time), He would once again *manifest His glory.* And so will He do likewise *in* and *for* and *through* us.

Fortunately they "listened to and obeyed the voice of the Lord their God [not vaguely or partly, but completely according] to the words of Haggai the prophet" (see verse 12 of the Amplified Bible). They examined themselves, repented, and got about God's business, repairing His house, the temple. Because of their obedience, the Spirit of God came upon Haggai to prophesy a greater glory, a greater revival or spiritual Feast of Tabernacles in the last days in which we live.

> **For thus saith the LORD of hosts; Yet once, it is a little while, and I *will* shake the heavens, and the earth, and the sea, and the dry land; And I will shake all nations, and the desire of all nations shall come: and I will fill this house with glory, saith the LORD of hosts. The silver *is* mine, and the gold *is* mine, saith the LORD of hosts. The glory of this latter house shall be greater than of the former, saith the LORD of hosts: and in this place will I give peace, saith the LORD of hosts. (Hag. 2:6-9)**

God the Father sent His Son as *the* latter house for our example. Now He is preparing the end-day bride to be that latter house too. The shaking has begun. Like these Jewish predecessors, God wants us to consecrate ourselves to Him and His purposes now. He has a huge house to build and fill up. It is His family built with living stones filled with His glory. And He can and will shake the whole earth to bring His Word to pass.

After these thirty days of introspection in the Hebrew sixth month of Elul, Teshuvah continues within the first ten days of the religious seventh month, Tishri.[19] A gathering of ten is called a *minyan* meaning "just enough to do God's business." **These final ten days of Teshuvah are called the "Ten Days of Awe."** They are considered the most holy days of the year. They start with a two-day Feast of Trumpets (Rosh Hashanah) and end

[19] Tishri (or Tishrei) is the first month of the Jewish civil and agricultural year and the seventh month of their ecclesiastical or religious year. The name is Babylonian. It usually occurs in September through October on our Gregorian calendar.

with the one Day of Atonement (Yom Kippur). The seven days in between are considered days when the heavens are opened to receive repentance. Though Tishri is the seventh month of the Hebrew religious calendar, it is also the *first* month of the Hebrew agricultural or civil calendar. So the Feast of Trumpets (Rosh Hashanah) is also Israel's civil New Year. And this agricultural first month[20] is most likely the *first month* of which Joel 2:23 prophesied that the former *and* latter rains would come together.

The original Ten Days of Awe were just that—awesome. On the original Feast of Trumpets (1-2 Tishri), Moses set up the tabernacle and placed all the furnishings within and without at the order of Jehovah God (Exod. 40:2, 17-30). This portable tent of old may have appeared modest and ordinary from the exterior, but within it was an extravagantly and skillfully fashioned multimillion-dollar throne room for Jehovah God. The cherubim and mercy seat were crafted in pure, refined gold. They were placed upon the gold-covered Ark of the Covenant. Three of the walls surrounding it were also covered with pure gold. However, despite its exquisite beauty, God promised to manifestly indwell it *only* if they followed His directions *exactly*. They did. As soon as Moses completed the move, God immediately responded by manifesting His presence as a brilliant Sh'khinah cloud with weighty glory.

> **Then a cloud covered the tent of the congregation, and the glory of the LORD filled the tabernacle. [35] And Moses was not able to enter into the tent of the congregation, because the cloud abode thereon, and the glory of the LORD filled the tabernacle** [Approximately 1688 BCE]. **(EXOD. 40:34-35)**

[20] This is why Exod. 40:2 refers to 1 Tishri as "the first day of the first month."

Jehovah's indwelling made this tent God's holy sanctuary on earth among men. Yet this was just the beginning of the month of the most holy Feasts of the Lord. It was a glorious and joyous beginning of the original Ten Days of Awe (1-10 Tishri). Later, that tent would be replaced by another for a season by King David and finally by Solomon's Temple. Regardless of the structure of God's sanctuary, Israel kept the Feast of Trumpets (Rosh Hashanah) with joy. As the psalmist wrote, "I had gone with the multitude, I went with them to the house of God, with the voice of joy and praise, with a multitude and kept holyday" (Ps. 42.4). Why joy? The joy of the Lord is Israel's strength (Neh. 8:10). Unfortunately, due to wide-spread and repetitive adulterous sin, the Temple was destroyed by the Babylonians, and Judah was taken captive. After seventy years in Babylon, they began to return to Jerusalem with two prominent leaders, Ezra and Nehemiah. Ezra, as a priest, led the first returning Jews back to Jerusalem. His vision was to reestablish praise and worship unto God by rebuilding the Temple (Ezra 3:4). Later Nehemiah arrived and united the residents to rebuild the gates and the wall around Jerusalem.

Upon completion they collectively kept the Feast of Trumpets with great joy. Both leaders chose to record that momentous time in history.

> **And when the seventh month was come, and the children of Israel were in the cities, the people gathered themselves together as one man to Jerusalem . . . From the first day of the seventh month** [1 Tishri] **began they to offer burnt offerings unto the LORD** [546-461BCE] **(Ezra 3:1, 6a) . . .**
>
> **And all the people gathered themselves together as one man . . . And Ezra the priest brought the law before the congregation both of men and women, and all that**

> **could hear with understanding, upon the first day of the seventh month** [1 Tishri]**. And he read . . . from the morning until midday . . . they bowed their heads, and worshipped the LORD with their faces to the ground . . . all the people wept, when they heard the words of the law. Then he said unto them, Go your way, eat the fat, and drink the sweet, and send portions unto them for whom nothing is prepared: for this day is holy unto our LORD: neither be ye sorry; for the joy of the LORD is your strength** [446-430BCE]. **(Neh. 8:1-3, 6, 10)**

Rosh Hashanah was always meant to be joyous but it was also meant to be holy. That particular year, Ezra had to steer the people to acknowledge their former sins also. He read the Scriptures to them. The Word brought profound conviction and ignited sincere repentance. Together they wept. But the Feast of Tabernacles was and still is intended to be a joyous feast, so Ezra instructed them *not* to focus on their sin but to rejoice in God's gracious forgiveness of their sin.

Likewise, the united bride of Christ gathering together before our Lord in praise and worship is vital to our preparation. Our praise should be jubilant, passionately expressing of our love for God, like David dancing before the Ark of the Covenant. It should be unashamed boasting of our Groom's holy attributes and all the redemptive work He accomplished for us. We rejoice for "the joy of the Lord is our strength" (Neh. 8:10) too. Collective worship is also essential; and it differs from praise. Worship is more reverential in attitude and action, a quiet bowing down or prostrating one's self to the very Word and Person of God. In this humble posture, together the bride may then tackle corporate sin and omission of duty through collective repentance. For when "we confess our sins He is faithful and just to forgive us our sins and cleanse us from all unrighteousness" (1 John 1:9). After confession we too may rejoice once again as Paul declared, "Rejoice in the Lord always and again I say, Rejoice" (Phil. 4:4).

Our individual Feast of Trumpets is our joyful new life in Christ washed clean by His blood. Collectively this feast is meant to awaken the church to her collective state in Christ and preparation for His return. Our collective praise and worship is powerful. It invites God's presence among us and beyond. And unity *commands* His blessings (Ps. 133:3), not just for us but also for those who live around us. And we don't have to limit gatherings to just those particular two days but at any and every God-inspired opportunity! **Collective gatherings of joyous praise to God previews and ultimately prepares us for our future rapture to heaven.**

In the original Ten Days of Awe (1-10 Tishri) God indwelt the tabernacle on the first Feast of Trumpets (1 Tishri). Then Moses beckoned all the congregation to repent of any personal sin and make an appropriate animal-blood sacrifice at the door of the tabernacle. They each had to kill an innocent animal by their own hands to experience the weight of their wrong-doing. Then the priests stepped in and sprinkled the blood on the altar and burnt the remains. They were called "offerings made by fire." This continued until the tenth day. Later, God added a national day of repentance, the Day of Atonement on 10 Tishri to cover the whole nation in years thereafter. On that day, the High Priest would sprinkle blood upon the mercy seat of the Ark of the Covenant for the sins of all Israel while all Israel fasted from food and water for twenty-four hours. This most holy day is the culmination of the forty days of Teshuvah.

Both **thirty** (the number for *consecration*) and **forty** (the number of *testing*, as in Teshuvah) are very significant in reference to personal and collective fasting. **Fasting is voluntary Teshuvah**, which is extremely impacting when directed by

God. Personal fasting aids our personal renewal, but the effect of collective fasting ordained by God *far* surpasses the personal benefits. Collective fasting leads to collective repentance. Collective repentance opens the floodgates of revival and triggers the continuous release of God's manifest miraculous power in the midst of whole congregations, communities, and even nations. This I learned under the tutelage of the Holy Spirit.

After my second trip to Toronto in 1995, the Lord had me fast solely on water during the first week of 1996. The following Sunday, the Spirit of God moved in apparent power. He was confirming to me that obedience in fasting permits Him to pour out His glory in our midst. Yet the next Sunday thereafter was once again spiritually *dry*. There was no anointing. Two months later, the Lord gave me another fast of five days on water from February 25 through March 1. On the third night (Wednesday, February 28), I had just rolled into bed as my husband left for his night job. As he shut the front door behind him, immediately the Spirit of God came tangibly upon me, hovering over my outstretched body, face to face. I repeatedly heard, "This Sunday I will begin to pour out My Spirit." I finally understood that He wanted me to write a message, so I got up and wrote as He dictated His words.[21]

> **02/28/96: This Sunday, I will begin to pour out My Spirit upon My people. It will be an awesome display of My power and might. Deliverance and healing will occur spontaneously throughout the sanctuary as I move from person to person and touch My people with My love and grace. It will be a sovereign move of My Spirit. The manifestations of My Spirit will shake My people . . . I encourage My people to seek My face and My presence as never before. In My presence they will**

[21] From then on I always kept a pen and paper available.

> **be delivered, healed, restored, renewed, revived, and equipped for the end-days ministry. Taste and see if I AM not as good as My word speaks of former years. I AM the same. I have not changed. My power has not diminished but rather I plan to display such works as to make the former seemingly small. This is My hour, saith the Lord. My fire is falling and purging and purifying for My Name's sake. I will have a people who walk righteous as well as being made righteous. I will have a people who will walk in the authority and power I have ordained from the foundation of the earth. I will be glorified throughout the earth in and through them. My anointing shall be increased in these latter days. And only those who will seek Me now will be able to operate in that anointing. I call My people to set time aside for Me consistently. And I will visit My people personally and individually as well as corporately. I will take back the spoils of darkness that are already Mine. Great will be My end-time revival! Greater than your imagination can fathom. Truly, truly** [of a certainty] **I will do it. I will perform it . . . so rejoice! The night will soon pass away, and the dawning of a new day is beginning in the birth pangs of the prayer of My saints. A day of glory for My church, My bride, My love. Be expectant. Believe and ye will prosper in all things, saith the Lord.**

I knew that I was to share this with my pastor, though I was reluctant to do so. I dodged him a few times, and finally he asked me if I had a word for him. So I read it to him in his office, and immediately, the Spirit of God fell on both of us with holy laughter. I couldn't wait to see what God had up His sleeve for that Sunday! The unfolding was far more exciting.

I arrived that Sunday morning in full anticipation. But I was asked to usher. I didn't want to usher; I didn't want to miss out on what God was going to do. Reluctantly, I agreed. As the praise ascended, I was at the front end of an aisle looking toward the back of the sanctuary when the *Lord came down that very aisle.* I didn't see Him with my physical eyes, but I saw Him. He blew right through me with immense force while I discerned an angel holding me up from my back as He passed on through me. (Without the angel, I would have fallen flat on the floor.) He then swept through the auditorium like a mighty wind. I cannot appropriately nor fully describe this visitation of His Spirit that day, but it was awesome! Through repetitive instruction I learned that with or without a message, He would move after every obediently-kept fast that *He* had chosen.

One time, I was given no choice. As I prayed that Tuesday morning in our sanctuary, the Lord gripped one of my legs and rolled me back and forth across the platform in the sanctuary. Then He spoke in fierce intonations His will and work for our transformation. I wrote it down as He spoke.

> **07/28/98: Sinner** [a believer like you and me] **in the hands of an angry God. Angry at sin . . . Angry at unbelief. Angry at indifference and striving and unfaithfulness in the things of God. My fire is about to fall . . . My people are not ready. Some will be consumed. Some will leave in fear. Some will call it false and . . . All because their hearts were not prepared. But those who have sought Me will humble themselves before Me and burn with passion for souls and the well-being of one another. They will link arms to win a city, to cross the** [harvest] **fields together, gathering a great harvest of lost souls. I will come in power and might. No more the meek Lamb but the violent Lion. I will roar . . . and My message** [will be] **of hope, yes, but a message of truth and purity and power, the power to cut back the evil veil even now hiding My Face from My people and the evil veil upon My people's hearts that** [has] **veiled My love to** [being seen by] **the masses. I am coming soon.**

> **Be prepared. Be ready. Stand firm on My word, My will, My purpose. Be not distracted or doubtful or fretful . . . Seek Me diligently 'till I come as FIRE. Wait upon Me and seek My truth; seek My heart and know My Ways. I love you and I love My people, but My wrath must consume wrong passions and lies. Hurts will surface. Ugliness in My people will surface. It will look like all-out war, a battlefield, a mess, but it is Me cleansing My people. Be ready, for I come sooner than you think, fiercer than you have ever known Me, sharper than a two-edged sword. I will work and I will spare none.** [I will leave none alone.] **I will convince all plainly of their sin. Then when the FIRE subsides and the pots are melted, I will reshape them into My image and likeness . . .**

He pinned me down for an involuntary three-day absolute fast. I left far more broken, willing, and obedient. His message was a must to share.

Every other month for over a year, He gave me a fast of five, seven, or ten days in length. When I obeyed God's voice in fasting, He moved in power! When I didn't, He didn't. And yet these personal fasts failed to *maintain* a move of God's Holy Spirit. Longer personal fasts of twenty-one, thirty, or forty days *did sustain* a move of God for a matter of weeks, but again, His glory would dwindle once the fast ended. Despite the span of the fast, I learned that fasting is only effective when He is Lord over it. We must let Him determine the timing, the length, and the type, and depend on His grace to accomplish it. We do not make it happen. We just ask and then obey His voice. Dr. Bill Bright, who is now in the presence of the Almighty, was compelled by God to call three million Christians to fast forty days before the year 2000 for nationwide revival.[22] I believe that quo-

[22] Bill Bright, *The Coming Revival* (Orlando, FL: New Life Publications, 1995).

ta was fulfilled.

These forty-day fasts and fervent prayer are part of our voluntary Teshuvah, a form of testing and cleansing for transformation. The narrative of the Mount of Transfiguration provides us with some insights regarding it. Transfiguration, in the Greek, is *metamorphoo*. It equates with the radical makeover of the caterpillar into a butterfly by way of its restrictive cocoon and its extremely difficult emergence from within it. Emerging from the cocoon requires excessive fluids being pressure-pumped into its new wings for flight. Jesus was transfigured (metamorphoo) on the Mount as He spoke of His coming suffering in crucifixion. And so, we have been promised to be changed (metamorphoo) from glory to glory into His very image as we behold Him (2 Cor. 3:18).

Is this impact in beholding Him while we are in victory and in triumph? Well, not so much as in Teshuvah. For we behold Him more clearly in difficulties, persecutions, fasting, and sufferings. There on the Mount, the glorious presence of God manifested analogous to His glorious indwelling of the tabernacle and temple. Jesus, Moses, and Elijah all shone with His radiant splendor. Peter (perplexed in his soul at the time) offered to (*do* something) build them booths or tabernacles. He did not recognize that the greatest factor of transformation is *being* in His fearful or loving presence. However, Peter did discern the association of the Feast of Tabernacles to the result of personal transformation. Jesus, Moses, and Elijah exemplify the Groom and His transformed bride, and they all have two common experiences. Each one fasted forty days and each one walked in vast apostolic power and authority, as will the bride who has made herself ready. But honestly, a forty-day fast is not a fixed prerequisite.

Interestingly, each of *their* forty-day fasts was initiated differently. Jesus was *driven* by the Spirit of God into the wilderness—a place void of God's splendor—to fast forty days and live on water only (Luke 4:1) in the presence of relentless evil: Satan. Upon finishing His fast, the Father sent angels to minister to Him. And He returned in the power of the Holy Spirit (Luke 4:14) for apostolic ministry, the ministry of Christ: preaching good news to the poor, restoring the broken-hearted, healing the physically sick, and delivering the captives (Luke 4:18). Twice, Moses (as a faithful remnant bride) was called up Mount Sinai by Jehovah to keep an absolute fast of no food or water for forty days in Jehovah's life-giving and sustaining presence. Moses obeyed and returned with great revelations from God. His face reflected the glory of the Lord while he carried within him the promises of a miraculous ministry and divine intercessory favor for the nation.

Elijah, however, was totally different. After an extraordinary victory over the false Baal prophets, divine fire rushing from heaven, and desperately needed rain returning to the land, Elijah *chose* to run into the wilderness from Jezebel and die. He appeared unfaithful and failing. But God met him where he was and sent an angel to serve him. Twice, Elijah ate a baked cake and drank a cruise (or jar) of water and "went in the strength of that meat [divine food] forty days and forty nights unto Horeb the mount of God" (1 Kings 19:8). Horeb means "dryness or desert." In fear, Elijah ran from Jezebel and God, but God graciously gave him a forty-day fast and governed its outcome. In the end, Elijah was sent to call out his successor, Elisha, and anoint the next king to rule over the ten northern tribes. Elisha later received, by faith, a double portion of the anointing upon Elijah and performed twice the number of recorded miracles as his predecessor. The bride, even those seemingly failing or defeated by the world's system today, will prevail in the power of God and even mentor a younger generation to excel in the miraculous. Through her intercession, Yahweh will reestablish national destinies and God-ordained and chosen civil government leadership.

Unlike Jesus (at least as recorded), Moses and Elijah both walked in the miraculous *before* they fasted forty days, and others did so without any evidence of a prolonged fast; therefore, the forty-day fast is not a prerequisite for all, but it will be an identifying feature for some. It should never be entered upon lightly but only after much prayer and confirmation. But when called by God, it produces incredibly grand results. For instance, each year from 1997 to 1999, the Lord called me to a forty-day denial fast of carrot juice and a soy protein drink daily, as I was very thin at the time. When I obeyed, there was an impressive sustained movement of His Spirit in our services throughout the span of the fast. During the last forty-day fast, a healing evangelist came to minister, and the miracles were incredibly more powerful than usual and many souls were saved.

One of those years, the second year, I did not fully cooperate. The fast started at the same time I began teaching a series on prayer. For a couple weeks, I did fine. His grace was more than sufficient, but then I rebelled and came off it. A couple days before I was to teach the next lesson, I fell very ill. For two days I lay in bed totally *out of it.* I was feverish and soaked with perspiration. But at 4 p.m. that Tuesday, the symptoms instantly lifted. The Lord firmly ordered me to get up, take a shower, and dress to teach. He told me that I now was where I should have been had I obeyed in fasting. The lesson went extremely well that night, and I finished that fast. From this I learned that God is a God of mercy and second chances. When we stray, we must repent and get up and go again, not dwelling on our disobedience and failing, but then not testing Him too far, either! Our aim must be high: an aim for willing obedience!

These fasts are one portion of our offerings and sacrifices before our God, whether short or long. And though a **thirty** or **forty**-day prolonged fast is not always necessary for us individually, it is *an absolute must* for the corporate body of Christ that He may manifest His glory in our services! It is part of our Teshuvah. Corporate fasting may require one meal each week for every member or one full day of a particular thirty or forty-day period for each member because the emphasis of the prophet Joel is repetitively *all* (Joel 1:14. 2:15-17). God calls *all* to participate. The Brownsville revival began shortly after a thirty-day corporate fast. Sometimes, even clusters of congregations or the city church will fast in unison. The more involved, the more powerful the move of God's Spirit *if* He initiated it. Individuals desperate for God may do more than the usual but only as He leads. Our intercessory team usually fasted more than the congregation in general. Often these eight dedicated ladies covered all the days among themselves. And God always honored our obedience, particularly in personal transformation that we might manifest His character and glory!

Ultimately, our transformation through Teshuvah culminates with the radiant beauty of holiness by which we are called to worship God (Ps. 29:2, 96:9; 1 Chron. 16:29). This is the utmost splendor, the magnificent comeliness of the bride of Christ made ready. This lovely attribute is not a minor detail, debatable option, or unreasonable request, but it is an absolute prerequisite for consistent and continual manifested union. God said, "Be ye holy; for I am holy" (1 Pet. 1:16). Only a holy bride can truly unite with a holy Groom in manifest power and glory. How else can we be our holy Beloved's and our holy Beloved be ours (Song of Sol. 6:3)? Certainly we are made holy in spirit by the blood of the Lamb the moment we (our spirits) are saved (1 Pet. 1:2), but holiness must penetrate and inundate our soul as well until it shapes every expression of our life toward others.

To reach this outcome requires Teshuvah, just as dirty chunks of coal need extreme pressure to become dazzling diamonds.

For Israel, holiness, or sanctification, was in the keeping of the ten obligations of the ketubah or written marriage contract. The first four commandments defined Israel's appropriate marital fellowship with Jehovah God (vertical) and entrance into His rest or trust. The last six (Exod. 20:12-17) defined Israel's suitable behavior toward one another (horizontal).

> **Honour thy father and thy mother: that thy days may be long upon the land which the LORD thy God giveth thee. Thou shalt not kill. Thou shalt not commit adultery. Thou shalt not steal. Thou shalt not bear false witness against thy neighbour. Thou shalt not covet thy neighbour's house, thou shalt not covet thy neighbour's wife, nor his manservant, nor his maidservant, nor his ox, nor his ass, nor any thing that is thy neighbour's. (Exod. 20:12-17)**

It sounds complicated, but it has always been simple. The love of God fulfills them all. What love? God-love, unconditional agape love, which, according to 1 Corinthians 13:4-8 (AMP) is patient and kind, thinks the best of every person, pays no attention to a suffered wrong, and more. This love doesn't covet another's spouse. This love doesn't covet another's belongings. This love doesn't slander the reputation of another with gossip. This love doesn't hurt or hate. Jesus explained that loving God and loving people fulfills all the law and the prophets (Matt. 22:37-40) and thereby keeps *all* our divine marital obligations.

Obedience to God includes walking in love as the God-ordained expression of our soul sanctification as His bride.

> **Seeing ye have purified your souls in obeying the truth through the Spirit unto unfeigned love** [agape] **of the**

> **brethren, see that ye love** [agape] **one another with a pure heart fervently. (1 Pet. 1:22)**

Our obedience to truth is summarized by our loving one another. It is "unfeigned," meaning "real, not artificial." The Lord does not want a Barbie doll bride that looks good on the outside but has nothing authentic inside her heart. That is why it requires such deep introspection and repentance in preparation. This obedient "agape-love" lifestyle also prepares us for His return.

> **God is love** [agape]**; and he that dwelleth in love** [agape] **dwelleth in God, and God in him. Herein is our love** [agape] **made perfect, that we may have boldness in the day of judgment: because as he is, so are we in this world. (1 John 4:16b, 17)**

If we are walking in love with one another and the lost in this world, we will not be ashamed at His coming. We will be confident, able to look Him in the eyes without turning away.

> **And the Lord make you to increase and abound in love** [agape] **one towards another, and towards all men, even as we do towards you: To the end he may stablish your hearts unblameable in holiness before God, even our Father, at the coming of our Lord Jesus Christ with all his saints. (1 Thess. 3:12-13)**

The bride truly walking in unconditional love has been made ready through purification and transformation.

The apostle Paul explained to the Thessalonians (1 Thess. 3:12-4:10) the correlation of three forms of love (agape, eros, and philia) in our soul sanctification. The agape love is God's unconditional love in which we are to live and breathe and have our being. The eros love refers to natural passion expressed in sexual intimacy. Philia love is brotherly affection. All are good within God's boundaries, but only agape love fulfills our divine marriage agreement. God declares that our sanctification, or holiness, requires that our eros love, or natural passions, *remain submitted to His agape love,* or holy passion, for Him. Within our walk of agape love toward one another, we may enjoy the natural eros passion with our wedded spouse with God's blessing. It is good. It is His gift to us. But outside of God's holy perimeter, eros love is sin, unclean and unholy (1 Thess. 4:3-7). Agape love will not commit adultery, "defrauding a brother" (verse 6). And agape love will not commit "fornication," which is sin against one's own body, His temple (as noted in verse 3, 1 Cor. 6:18).

Brotherly, or philia love is also good. It is defined as fraternal love, or tender affection, and includes philanthropy or benevolence toward mankind. The Father has tender affection for His Son (John 5:20, 17:26) and for us (John 16:27). But it, like eros love, is but a minute fraction of His all-encompassing agape love. It is within our walk of agape love toward one another that will compel us also to be kindly affectionate and generous, showing compassion on the poor and downcast, bettering our society, and supporting caring institutions. All forms of love will prevail in sincerity in our lives and relationships as long as His agape love abounds *in* us and flows *through* us.

Is this something we must *do*? Not in our own strength. We must desire transformation, but ultimately, our horizontal walk in love develops from our vertical relationship (and fellowship) with God, who *is* love. The Father commanded all mankind to enter into this love relationship with Christ through faith (1 John 3:23a). And then His Son commanded all in that relationship with Him were to love one another (1 John 3:23b). Faith gets us in the Vine but agape love is the way *of* the Vine (John 15:12). But as simple as it is, this is a command we cannot keep in our own strength. The ability to love one another comes from loving our Lord. As we cleave to Christ, we leave the world and its power over us, and thereby, win the world to Him. What begins as sweet fellowship with our Lord spills over with love for one another, whether family or stranger, friend or foe (Matt.5:43), believer or unbeliever. And this love for one another is the evidence that will convince the world that we are truly His disciples (John 13:34-35) and set us apart *from* the world *before* the world!

Just as the alabaster box must be broken in order to release the sweet smell of the perfume within it, so must we be broken to release His fragrant love deposited within our spirit (Rom. 5:5). It is in the midst of our greatest Teshuvah that we are broken or pressed out like the transformed butterfly emerging from its cocoon. All the anger, rebellion, hardness, and rudeness is removed in the tightened squeeze, and all that remains is the pure essence of His love-nature. For God *is* love, and perfect love lives in us. Through our transformation, we will mount up with wings as the eagles and soar in the heavenlies aloft by the Spirit of love regardless of the madness and sin that abounds around us. We are His "kingdom of priests and holy nation," testifying of His goodness and glory. Those of the world will always takes note of extraordinary people with respect, Nobel Prizes, and good reviews, but our Lord will bestow an even greater honor upon His bride made ready—His manifested glory. This Christ in us is our hope of His glory (Col. 1:27), His glory rising up from within us (Isaiah 60:1) in these last dark days. And it is the beaming splendor of our transformation in Christ (the beauty of holiness) that will bring nations to their knees for Christ.

There are five days between the Day of Atonement and the Feast of Tabernacles. *Five is the number of grace.* No matter how much we fast and watch, we will *never* earn or deserve revival! We will *never* earn or deserve to walk in the miraculous! It is all by the grace and faithfulness of our Lord. Let's keep these feasts as the Holy Spirit leads us.

CHAPTER 7

FLOOD OF GLORY

And thou shalt observe . . . the feast of ingathering at the year's end. (Exod. 34:22)

This feast of ingathering is better known as the Feast of Tabernacles (*Succoth* or *Sukkot*). It finalizes and celebrates the greater latter harvest season of ancient agricultural Israel. Like the Feast of Unleavened Bread, it encompasses seven days in length (15-21 Tishri) and then is followed by a one-day feast called *Shemini Atzeret* on 22 Tishri. Together, seven plus one equals eight, the number of new beginnings, for in these last days, there will be a new beginning of apostolic power and authority in ministry. Signs and wonders will accompany the called-out ones, "His wife," or bride, that "hath made herself ready" (Rev. 19:7). Keeping the Feast of Tabernacles coincides with the manifested union of Christ and His bride in the approaching greater outpouring of God's Spirit of which Joel termed the "former and latter rain" together (Joel 2:23b). This great outpouring is right on our horizon. And we anticipate that our participation will be in the fullness of the promise of the Spirit—a global flood of God's glory and an unprecedented global harvest of souls!

On the first day of this original seven-day feast, Moses escorted Aaron and his four sons into the tabernacle to remain in God's presence (Exod. 40:34-35). Aaron and his sons remained in the tabernacle for seven days (15-21 Tishri). This was their consecration and sanctification to obediently minister as priests before God's face for the benefit of God's people (Lev. 8:33). On that eighth day (Shemini Atzeret), Aaron and his sons had finally come out of the Lord's tabernacle. Moses addressed the entire nation of Israel twice promising that God would appear saying, "To day the Lord will appear unto you" (Lev. 9:4). "The glory of the Lord shall appear unto you" (Lev. 9:6). And after proper sacrifices and offerings were made, He did! Jehovah God's response was awe-inspiring to all.

> **And Aaron lifted up his hand toward the people, and blessed them, and came down from offering of the sin offering, and the burnt offering, and peace offerings. And Moses and Aaron went into the tabernacle of the congregation, and came out, and blessed the people: and the glory of the LORD appeared unto all the people. And there came a fire out from before the LORD, and consumed upon the altar the burnt offering and the fat: which when all the people saw, they shouted, and fell on their faces. (Lev. 9:22-24)**

The Lord God not only accepted the sacrifices of that day with His holy fire; He also accepted the priests who were to minister before Him. From this point on, God was willing to eternally dwell among His covenant people on earth in their midst. His glory would never depart from their midst if they remained obedient. From that day on, God's presence was manifested continually throughout their forty years in the wilderness and generations beyond. Then His appearance was "off and on" depending on their obedience. Unfortunately His Sh'khinah glory finally departed due to Israel's continual spiritual adultery from this tabernacle (1 Sam. 4:21) and later from Solomon's temple

(Ezek. 10).

Our keeping the Feast of Tabernacles is primarily yielding to Christ in us to display our holy union. He has accepted us as His bride and royal priesthood to minister within His supernatural realm displaying His glory, fire and miraculous power.

> **But ye are a chosen generation, a royal priesthood, an holy nation, a peculiar people; that ye should shew forth the praises of him who hath called you out of darkness into his marvellous light. (1 Pet. 2:9)**

> **And hath made us kings and priests unto God and his Father; to him be glory and dominion for ever and ever. Amen. (Rev. 1:6)**

Yet proper sacrifices in obedience are still required. Hear and obey. Do it His way. Once made ready and purified by His fire, we will be a terror to darkness and brilliant escape light to those still in darkness. We are on the brink of this greater outpouring of God's Spirit, "the former and the latter rain" (Joel 2:23b). Those ready will participate in the fullness of the promise of the Spirit amid the global flood of God's glory! Signs and wonders will accompany His *wife* or bride that "hath made herself ready" (Rev. 19:7). This is not limited to the five-fold ministry, TV evangelists, famous teachers, and megachurch pastors but every passionate believer.

After returning from my first visit to the Brownsville revival, I caught a glimpse of this coming flood of God's glory in our sanctuary on Friday, August 30, 1996. The waters I saw (with eyes open) reached within a couple feet of our eighteen-foot ceiling. This great body of water was not peaceful and still; it was rather turbulent with churning forceful waves. Within my first twenty-one-day fast, I heard this word and quickly wrote it down as the Lord spoke to my heart:

09/05/96: There is coming a mighty deluge of My Glory. But this time, I will not seal you within an ark, but you will flow with and be apart of the deluge. Righteousness will surface and prevail. Sin will sink to the dark chambers of the bottom sea. My wind will blow to recede the waters. You will be lifted out, and all that will remain is miry sludge. The fire of justice will burn it to parchness, and it will blow away like chaff. The institutions of this world order will crumble to the nothingness they were founded upon. Only those institutions founded on My cornerstone that I have laid will endure for eternity. And I will return then to the earth with My glorified saints. The deluge is coming soon. Be ready to swim with My Spirit. It will be a strong current of My Spirit so strong that many of My own who has swum in past outpourings may not recognize it at first, but the fruit will prove it. Be ready. Purify your hearts. Purify your souls. I call for holiness, for I AM a holy God. And only the righteous will prevail and surface. Those in sin will sink with the world. Like quicksand, the world will pull them down and clutch their souls. Be ready, My people. Be holy as I AM holy, saith the Lord. Be ready to war and battle for souls, for the time is short. The time is short. Turn from your sins.

The flood of His Spirit is coming! Let's get ready to flow with Him! This is the New Covenant Feast of Tabernacles before His return.

We, as His New Covenant *living* tabernacles, have been wondrously wrought, knit under His close scrutiny and direction in the wombs of our natural mothers. We are eternal spirits clothed in humble flesh, but God wills to manifest His glorious presence *within* us and *through* us individually and collectively as He did with His Son Jesus. The lovesick bride yearns to experience His manifest presence from within but also His train filling our sanctuaries and weighing down His priests once again.[23] That too is the Feast of Tabernacles! It is the ongoing manifested presence of God! As the awakened bride of Christ and "holy priesthood," this requires that we also "offer up spiritual sacrifices acceptable to God by Jesus Christ" (1 Pet. 2:5),[24] not just fasting and prayer, but more. King David defined one of singular importance:

> **My sacrifice [the sacrifice acceptable] to God is a broken spirit; a broken and a contrite heart [broken down with sorrow for sin and humbly and thoroughly penitent], such, O God, You will not despise. (PS. 51:17, AMP; BRACKETS IN THE ORIGINAL)**

God is looking for broken hearts, contrite hearts, humble hearts, and thoroughly penitent hearts, which will burn in passion for Him as the fire of the Holy Ghost *falls* and the glory of the Lord *appears*. His glory will be discernible *but not to all.* The historian, Josephus, made a selective remark in his account referring to God's indwelling the tabernacle.

> **The sky was clear, but there was a mist over the tabernacle only, encompassing it, but not with such a very deep and thick cloud as seen in the winter season, nor yet in so thin a one as men might be able to discern anything through it; but from it there dropped a sweet dew and such a one as showed the presence of God to those that desired it and believed it. (Josephus 3.8.5. (203))**

Imagine that! Not everyone saw His glory cloud! Only the watchful remnant that desires God's presence and believes will see His greater anointing flow *unto* and *through* them.

[23] "Glory" literally means "heavy" or "weighty," in a good sense.

[24] This includes offerings, which are voluntary, as well as sacrifices, which are necessary.

After King David established Jerusalem as the capital city of Israel, his son Solomon built the temple. Israel dedicated Solomon's temple for seven days and then celebrated the Feast of Tabernacles for another seven days. God, the Almighty, omnipotent Jehovah, Creator of heaven and earth, chose *to indwell* once again a natural structure made by frail human hands, as He had done before in the tabernacle. Scripture provides two perspectives of this revival.[25] Note the Old Covenant sacrifices being joined and upgraded with the type of New Covenant sacrifices of praise, thanks, and worship.

> **Also the Levites *which* were the singers, all of them of Asaph, of Heman, of Jeduthun, with their sons and their brethren, being arrayed in white linen** [like the bride], **have cymbals and psalteries, and harps, stood at the east end of the altar, and with them an hundred and twenty priests sounding with trumpets) It came even to pass, as the trumpeters and singers were as one, to make one sound to be heard in praising and thanking the LORD; and when *they* lifted up *their* voice with the trumpets and cymbals and instruments of musick, and praised the LORD, *saying*, For he is good; for his mercy *endureth* for ever: that *then* the house was filled *with* a cloud, even the house of the LORD; So that the priests could not stand to minister by reason of the cloud: for the glory of the LORD had filled the house of God. (2 Chron. 5:12-14)**

David had hired 288 singers and 4,000 musicians to praise and give thanks before the Lord continually while the ark was

[25] Note that the singers and musicians of the Tabernacle of David (a type of New Covenant believers and our ministry) merged with the furnishings and service of the Old Covenant priests much like the twenty-four elders before the throne of God in heaven. Twelve is the number of divine government or divine order. So the twenty-four is God uniting the twelve tribes (the Old Covenant people) with the twelve disciples (the New Covenant people) before His throne.

placed in a tabernacle on Mt. Zion when he ruled from Jerusalem. But this day was many years later. This mass of worshippers was far greater in number, for their sons and brothers joined them. One hundred twenty trumpets alone was staggering. Yet they became one in their worship.

King Solomon offered up a prayer of dedication. In response, God again accepted the natural blood sacrifices of the Old Covenant but also the spiritual sacrifices of praise and worship of the coming New Covenant in Jesus.

> **Now when Solomon had made an end of praying, the fire came down from heaven, and consumed the burnt offering and the sacrifices; and the glory of the LORD filled the house. [2] And the priests could not enter into the house of the LORD, because the glory of the LORD had filled the LORD's house. [3] And when all the children of Israel saw how the fire came down, and the glory of the LORD upon the house, they bowed themselves *with their faces* to the ground upon the pavement, and worshipped, and praised the LORD, saying, For he is good; for his mercy endureth for ever** [Approximately 1,000 BCE]. (**2 Chron. 7:1-3**)

Josephus wrote that "*God gladly pitched his tabernacle therein*" and His fire of acceptance came "*running out of the air and rushed with violence upon the altar, in the sight of all, and...consumed the sacrifices*" [8.4.4. (118)]. Jehovah again passionately came with fervor for Israel. God wanted this union with Israel far more than they did! He was so ready and willing to be one with her and still is. The passion of Christ for His bride is just as intense! Will we obey His Word that He might perform it?

On that eighth day, Shemini Atzeret (22 Tishri), Jehovah appeared to King Solomon in the night and shared with him the warning signs of His people in adultery. He purposefully gave these words to later awaken His beloved Israel and also the church in future generations, for He already knew the church (like Israel) would sleep around with the world, sin, and permit His manifest glory to depart. So He declared, "If I shut up heaven that there be no rain, or if I command the locusts to devour the land, or if I send pestilence among my people; If my people, which are called by my name, shall humble themselves, and pray, and seek my face, and turn from their wicked ways; then will I hear from heaven, and will forgive their sin, and will heal their land" (2 Chron. 7:13-14).

God must permit the heavens (rain clouds) to shut when His bride is unfaithful to the marriage covenant, that is, when disobedience (sin) replaces obedience to His written and spoken Word. The lack of rain in the natural is just one sign confirming the lack of His glorious manifest presence and the many blessings of health, prosperity, peace, plenty, and rest. This closed heaven (also called a brass or iron heaven), the locusts, and the pestilence are each one portion of the five cycles of increasing discipline recorded in Leviticus chapter 26 and Deuteronomy chapter 28. They are within the Mt. Sinai marriage covenant as the consequence of Israel's infidelity. God is consistent and unchanging. Sin brings judgment to Israel and the church. Yes, we are redeemed "from the curse of the law" by the precious blood of the Lamb (Gal. 3:13). But only when we *repent* from sin is the curse attached to that sin canceled. Sinners are not responsible for brass heavens, saints are. Only we can reverse it by repenting of *our* spiritual adultery, complacency, and wrong priorities and then returning to Him and keeping our marriage vow of undivided love.

A brass heaven refers to continual lack of rain, drought so severe that vegetation dies, and fires go on a rampage of destruction. It is a curse usually pointing to the church's disobedience as forewarned by Moses (Deut. 28:23-24) and the prophet Joel (Joel 1:10, 12, 19-20). Regular rain and snow in moderation is a great blessing of God that He wills to provide us, but only our obedience to Him secures these blessings for us. Their lack means judgment. Yet excessively heavy rain and raging hazardous storms can also imply judgment. I grew up along the Mississippi River, where floods were sometimes catastrophic. Certainly New Orleans with Katrina and the northern East Coast with Hurricane Sandy clearly reveal the destructive power of floodwater. And floods seem to be escalating in frequency and power. But they are also previews for us of the great flood of the Holy Spirit coming in overpowering strength and wondrous display! Rain, in moderation, represents God's provision and blessing, but floods do not.

In the vile and wicked days in which Noah lived, Jehovah God sent a furious flood of water as *judgment* upon the whole earth. It was as a tumultuous cleansing of wickedness amid massive destruction. Though the righteous were safe and secure within the ark, it too heaved and shook and groaned upon the churning surface of floodwater. God's chosen place of preservation was not easy. It was dark, dreary, and difficult. So will it be for the end-day bride. The end-day outpouring of His glory will emerge like floodwater. Floodwater is rapid and raging, a powerful force without restraint. It sweeps over every object in its path with great force, uprooting everything not anchored deeply in a sure foundation, sweeping away every hint of filth and debris from surfaced objects, and stirring up dark chasms of sludge and putrid matter. It is gruesome, but through it, God accomplishes very much very quickly, and a new beginning emerges as it recedes! God has promised mankind that He will never again send a flood of natural water over all the earth. The rainbow is His token of promise. But through the prophets Isaiah and Habakkuk, He declares, "The earth shall be filled with the knowledge of the glory of the LORD, as the waters cover the sea" (Hab. 2:14). A flood of His Spirit and revelation is coming. And a flood of God's glory is far more terrible than any flood of water!

This flood of God's glory will be extensively destructive toward evil in metropolises and certainly elsewhere, also! Should the saints bare our hearts to Him, His flood of glory will cleanse sin (whether in deed or attitude) from our lives, our streets, our higher learning centers, our marketplaces, our courts, governments, and institutions, and, yes, our congregations and theology. Every type of filth and flaw will be aggressively impacted. Drug dealing, anger, malice, murder, racism, adultery, theft, greed, pornography, addictions (alcohol, heroin, etc.), fetal murder, etc., will be flushed from its path. Prisons and brothels will be stripped clean. The putrid, hidden acts of molestation, human trafficking, perversion, and depravity will be laid bare before our Holy, Almighty God and then blasted away.

Yet in this violent upheaval, receptive hearts will be transformed from hard unproductive clay to fertile soil, like the banks of the Mississippi after floodwaters recede. Sprouts of life will emerge suddenly, like mushrooms after a spring rain. Harvest fields of souls will flourish as greedy businessmen become accountable to the poor with benevolent generosity as the proud are humbled, as the once-corrupt embrace moral ethics, as fathers return to their children and children return to their fathers, as batterers stop battering; and as married couples honor their vows. Peace, joy, and faith will steadily rise with the increase of newly-saved souls. Overall, the pliable will be purified, prepared, and passionate for the Lord. But hearts that resist our Lord's work will be hardened all the more, going deeper and deeper into darkness.

There is no question that this flood is approaching; the signs are clear. It is not a matter of *will* He come, it is a matter of whether our hearts *will be ready* to flow with Him *when* He comes. Have we dealt with the evil that lurks within our own souls? Have we anchored our souls in His Word? Have we come to know Him intimately that we may have confidence in His love regardless of the raging waves about us? Are we fully submitted to His will and sovereign work in our lives? Like the five wise virgins, we must stay filled with His oil to enter in when He comes and shine forth His glory. Like Mary, we must choose the better portion of extravagant fellowship with the Lord, even though the world, money, fame, occupation, and even worthy ministry scream for our constant attention. As living temples, we must become a place of prayer or continual communion with Him, carrying His loving presence wherever we go. We must abide in the Vine. Then, as we, His helpmeet, pray and declare His Word by faith: signs, wonders, and healings will follow us (Matt. 21:12-14), for we will be like Him at His appearing (1 John 3:2).

Obedience in watches, fasting, repentance, and prayer are the offerings and sacrifices that prepare us for this feast. But how do we actually *keep* this Feast of Tabernacles (15-21 Tishri) and Shemini Atzeret (22 Tishri), this place of manifested union with Christ? Like the Feast of Trumpets—with joy! The Feast of Tabernacles is called "the feast of joy." Hundreds of times the word "keep" is used in the Old Testament Scriptures, but only one Hebrew verb, *chagag*, is used exclusively in reference to keeping the feasts. Of the ten times chagag is used, twice it is for Passover and only once in reference to all the feasts. But it is used *seven times* for the Feast of Tabernacles. Chagag has a clear connection to this feast. To chagag means "go around in a circle, leaping and dancing, especially in a public assembly." That's right, in front of everyone! Like David before the Ark of the Covenant as he brought it to Mt. Zion in Jerusalem.

In May of 1996, God sent me to Israel for **twenty-one** days. I lived among Messianic Jews the first five days, participated in a Christian prayer tour for ten days, and finally spent the last week in an Arab hotel on the Mount of Olives overlooking the East Gate of old Jerusalem. While on the tour, one of the ladies invited me to Ruth Ward Heflin's home church. Heflin's congregants entered into a circular dance certain that God's glory would fall somewhere in the city of Jerusalem in response. Later, they would read about it in the paper. As they danced that night, I and other visitors stayed apart. We did not want to disturb them, yet God's presence was very tangible and weighty.

Later I read Heflin's book *Glory*. She described how to dance the glory of God down to earth specifically by a group dancing in a circle. According to Hebrew custom this is *the bridal dance*! Right before revival came to Brownsville, Heflin had taught this form of intercession there. Later that very year, in early November, eleven intercessors and I from our congregation joined the Brownsville intercessors in worship warfare dancing in a circle around the map of Pensacola. I never taught or promoted this dance, but ever since then I have witnessed intercessors, without plan or design, occasionally come together and dance hand in hand in a circle. Sometimes, individual intercessors twirl in their own circle. It should make one dizzy but rarely does. It is the bridal dance! Again, like David before the ark, this exuberant, unashamed dance is one way that we keep this feast of joy that His glory may fall in our community or region.

The joy of this feast ultimately manifests God's glory *upon* us and *through* us in our personal life, our ministry, and our collective gatherings. Jesus foretold this right on the feast days.

> **Now the Jew's feast of tabernacles was at hand . . . Now about the midst of the feast Jesus went up into the temple, and taught . . . In the last day, *that* great day of the**

> **feast, Jesus stood and cried, saying, If any *man* thirst, let him come unto me, and drink. He that believeth on me, as the scripture hath said, out of his belly shall flow rivers of living water. (But this spake he of the Spirit, which they that believe on him should receive: for the Holy Ghost was not yet *given*; because that Jesus was not yet glorified.) (John 7:2,14,37-39)**

Jesus went up to Jerusalem (a type of bride) to celebrate the Sukkot. During the middle of the eight days, He taught in the temple, the structure that demonstrated His ideal of union or oneness with us individually and collectively. Then He spoke out on the last or seventh day of Sukkot or the Feast of Tabernacles (**21** Tishri), which is called *Hoshana Rabbah,* meaning "the great hosanna" or "the great salvation."[26] Jesus called and still calls all that thirst to come drink of Him receiving the personal "well of water springing up into everlasting life" (John 4:14). Such is the salvation message, for the salvation of souls is a key part of revival. Yet it is also the call to the church to come closer to Him for the "rivers of living water" (John 7:38), the outpouring of His Spirit from within us. Immersed in His river, we can display His miraculous love and power—our manifested union with Him.

Jesus was probably teaching right as the priests were performing a special ceremony called *Simchat Beit HaShoevah*, the rejoicing of water pouring. This ceremony took place every day of Sukkot except the first day, 15 Tishri. It was especially emphasized on the last or seventh day, **21** Tishri! The priests went out to the Water Gate to the pool of Siloam. There, the high priest drew the water known as *living water* into a golden vessel.

[26] Salvation, which is the meaning of Jesus' name, is defined as healing, deliverance, wholeness, and restoration in both the Hebrew and Greek languages.

An assistant also held a vessel of wine. In Edward Chumney's book *The Seven Festivals of the Messiah,*[27] he writes that the people would then sing a song which went: "with joy we will draw water out of the wells of salvation." Also before the wine and water were poured out at the horn of the brazen altar, the priests set branches of willow to form a *chupah*, or wedding canopy! As the water was poured out, the people cried, "Hosanna," meaning, "save us" as they circled the altar once every day (16-20 Tishri). But on the seventh day, **21** Tishri, they circled the altar seven times, crying out for salvation, "Hosanna, save us." It was a bridal dance.

They were acting out the desired arrangement of God and His church, especially the end-day bride. The brazen altar is a type of cross. The wine represented marriage, joy, covenant, and blood. Marriage is a blood covenant, the cutting of which brings great joy to the two in union. So it is with Christ and His bride. Water and blood poured out of the side of our Lord at His death on the cross. And just as Eve was taken out of the first Adam's side as He slept, the bride of Christ was formed from Jesus' side as He *slept* three days in the earth. And because she is taken out *from* His side, she will walk *by* His side, for the two are one. This union is the means by which He continues to pour out these rivers of living water *through* us. Not just our personal well of salvation, but rivers with the potential to quench the thirst of multitudes! It is His resurrection power resident within us. He was the golden vessel, but in these last days, the bride, in union with Him, is becoming "His vessel of honor" fitted for honorable use in His house (2 Tim. 2:20), paralleling His own life and ministry in the earth.

The Lord granted me a glimpse of this manifested union while

[27] Edward Chumney, *The Seven Festivals of the Messiah* (Shippensburg, PA: Treasure House Publishers, 1994), 155-186.

I was in Argentina in July 1997. On the **twenty-first** day of the month, one participant was impressed to read Haggai 2:9, originally written by the Haggai on **21** Tishri, concerning the glory of the latter house. I knew that the seventh solar month of July was not the religious seventh Hebrew month, but God didn't seem to mind.[28] He was declaring that He was about to break open the heavens over the city of San Nicolas that coming week and provide an explosion of miracles through His bride at the scheduled Prayer Fair, Saturday, July 26, in the city's main park. It was there, the latter rain began to fall, and the Lord permitted me to preview this marital union with Christ, the miraculous, the Feast of Tabernacles in action *through* us!

I had been inspired to repeatedly ask for the working of miracles, gifts of healing, and the gift of faith for a couple days before the fair. That is not my usual prayer. Just an hour or so prior to the fair's start, the Lord gave me a prophetic word to pronounce over each of the seven prayer stations with three other intercessors I met from all across the USA. At the healing station I proclaimed, "All that came to Him were healed." (Weeks later, at home, I reread all the gospels which confirmed that He did, in fact, heal *everyone that came or was brought to Him!*) That was the station in which I was led to participate. As the first Argentine lady walked up to me, the Great Physician spoke very clearly to me, "She's not coming to you, she's coming to Me." My mouth dropped open. He was saying to me that *He* was going to heal everyone I prayed for that day. He was going to operate through me and He did.

The first lady and I looked at one another face to face. I had no

[28] Overall, the seventh solar month, **July**, became a personal Tishri for me. In the first days of July 1996, I had a visitation from the Lord, which represented my personal Rosh Hashanah. On July 10, 1993, my father died. It was my personal Yom Kippur. My trip to Argentina and ministry at the Prayer Fair in 1997 was my personal Feast of Tabernacles.

interpreter as of yet and couldn't speak more than a phrase or two of Spanish. But that was to my advantage. There was nothing to intimidate me. No one knew me and I knew no one. I pointed to myself and shook my head "no." I pointed toward heaven and shook my head "yes" with a smile. She smiled back. I laid hands on her and prayed simply but boldly, and the power of God fell on both of us. When the prayer was over, she was beaming and shaking her head affirmatively. Then another woman came and pointed to her left ear and the glands under her chin. I put my right index finger into her ear and the last three fingers under her chin and prayed, looking to God. His power fell so strongly that we both became drunk and were laughing in the Spirit. She enjoyed His presence and would not let go of me for some time. When she did, she pointed with a smile to her ear, which was very noticeably red and hot.

Soon an interpreter, seventeen-year-old Leona from the city of La Plata, began to assist me. Several people I ministered to were in pain, some in constant pain, which doctors could not treat. All of them left without pain. For one lady, I commanded the spirit of pain to leave and told her when the pain returned to rebuke it immediately in Jesus' name. For another, I only prayed for healing. When I finished she said there was still some pain, so I prayed again and it all left. For yet another one, I just laid my hands upon her. All three pain victims were healed. How did I know to minister to each one differently? I didn't, but *Christ in me* did! We were working in unison. We were one. It was almost as though I was watching Him work through me. One gentleman had observable skin cancer on his face. I put my hands right on it. Pastor Emil Hildebrand, the president of the united group of pastors of San Nicolas and the one to whom I was drawn to support in prayer, put his hand on my back to assist me. The skin of his face began to move like ocean waves. God was letting me know it was done.

Pastor Hildebrand then thrust me over to join a couple of believers praying for another man. I laid hands on him without looking, praying briefly. Nothing happened. Then I inquired of the Christian in charge what was wrong with the man. He told me that the man's former wife was a witch, and she had put curses on him. It was then that I glanced up at the man's face. The oppression was extremely obvious. With one hand on him, a groan poured out of my belly. He fell to the ground, then I got on my knees and touched his right hand, his forehead, his left hand, his left foot, and then his right foot, each time saying, "The blood of Jesus." As soon as I was done he was completely delivered. I did not know what I was doing because *I was not doing it!* Union was in operation. This glorious union went on for hours.

As it slowed up, another North American couple asked me how things had gone. When I told them God had healed everyone, they literally grabbed my hand and pulled me over to a very heavy-set Argentine woman sitting on a bench. They explained that the cartilage was missing in her right hip joint and that she was in great pain. I knew this would require a creative miracle, but instantly the Lord brought to my remembrance His rhema promise, "All that came to Him were healed!" So I put my left hand over her right hip area and commanded the cartilage back. I could feel Him working inside her, and from the expression on her face, she felt it also. She leaped up with a radiant smile while I stood in total awe of my gracious God. I felt overwhelming humility that He would use the likes of me. I am nobody. We are all nobodies. But for some reason, the Great Somebody wants to work in union with us. I will never forget that day! Its memory is the perpetual carrot outstretched before me. It keeps me going forward to claim my destiny as a child of God coming to my full maturation (Rom. 8:19). I will never be satisfied until I live continually in the Feast of Tabernacles. It is not just a season to gather together, though we probably will on these special dates for conferences, celebrations, prayer gatherings, etc. But for the New Covenant believers, it is meant to be an ongoing manifestation of *Christ in us* before a lost and dying world amid the greatest revival of worldwide history!

Alas, the next day I was *normal*. The North American couple asked for prayer for the husband's headache, but nothing happened! It is not us! I grieved that my experience of manifested union was so brief. He countered my despair and spoke these words to me:

> **07/29/97: I have come and I am coming. I have healed and I am healing. I have spoken and I am speaking. Don't put Me in your box. Let Me explode out the ends of your box. Don't limit Me, for I am limitless. I AM. I am the same: yesterday, today, and tomorrow. I have not changed, I am not changing. I am the same. Don't limit Me; I am limitless. I am infinite in power. I surpass all understanding, so lay your speculations and expectations of Me at My feet and permit Me to rule and reign in your life, in your fellowship,** [and] **in your society. I have spoken and I continue to speak with the same power, with the same authority which I exercised in Bible times. For the times of My wonders and miracles have not ceased, but I await to perform** [them] **as never before. Will you let Me? Will you lay down your desires and pursue Mine? Will you lay down your passions and take on Mine? You will see and experience and know the miraculous if you step out of My way and give Me the right of way: if you exist to let Me live through you. If you let Me BE. And you will never be ashamed. Never. The world will flock to My empowered church. The world will flock to My beautiful bride. The world will bow** [their knee] **at My feet. Choose your priorities: Me or you. Which shall it be? I will to do and will do as**

> **much as you permit Me. No less, no more. The choice is yours. Do you want Me, church? Seek Me while I may be found. Draw near to Me. Be spent with My life. Receive My living water, fresh from the well: new water for the thirsty soul. Life-giving water to draw dead souls to Me—for there is My heartbeat. My heart beats: none lost, none lost, none lost. All saved, all saved, all saved. Let My heart be transplanted into you. Never the same. Never the same. Never the same.**

This is our Feast of Tabernacles, the end-day compassionate, miraculous, soul-winning, body-healing walk of Christ in us, through us! Are you ready for this great revival? Let's keep the feasts, not by the letter of the law, but by His Spirit. Yet there is coming a day when every nation that came against Israel must annually send delegates to Jerusalem to keep the Feast of Tabernacles as do the Jews (Zech. 14:16-17), or their nation will receive no rain. And there is nothing wrong with joining Israel in the natural feasts either. But don't settle for those alone. Aim to carry His manifest presence wherever you go. Let Him auspiciously tabernacle His glory in and through you.

CHAPTER 8

THREE REVIVING SEASONS

Over two decades, without foreknowledge or plan, I noticed an increasing portion of the body of Christ consistently keeping the feasts[29] via united gatherings and outreaches (locally, regionally, nationally, and even globally). During those years God spoke to my heart numerical cues for the unfolding of His grand finale outpouring of His Spirit (Joel 2:23, 28) that we might expectantly prepare to reap a vast harvest of souls within three reviving seasons. On the eighth day of January 1999 (eight being the number for new beginnings), the Lord spoke to me a couple numerical signals concerning His divine timing and methodology.

> **01/08/99: Be it known unto you that I have not delayed. My timing is perfect. Be not fearful, nor doubt. For I have the season** [kairos] **within My hand. I hold the clock of My timing. I will release the tide of My Spirit and it will rise as I choose. Twenty-one (21) is the number. Search it out to know My will . . . I will flood this place and this city as I have promised . . . It is a corpo-**

[29] Using my prophetic journal in comparison with Arthur Spier, *The Comprehensive Hebrew Calendar 5660-5850, 1900-2100,* 3rd ed. (Jerusalem, New York: Feldheim Publishers, 1986), 1994-2012 (5755-5773).

> **rate move that I have designed, and** [I have] **prepared the hearts of My people to hear My voice and go forth. Many will not hear for they have pursued the world and pleasure, but My Gideon army will arise. And they are mighty in My eyes . . . This is the Jubilee (50) . . . though your preparation has been minuscule, My muscle will be great! All power is in Me. You have no might of your own. I will perform My word alone but though My people. They are straws through which I will flow. A straw is nothing but an agent of delivery.**

Immediately thereafter, I heard a numerical equation: **40 + 21 = 61**. He brought it before me again and again over several months to maintain my attention to it.[30]

God's equation announces that Teshuvah (**40**) will precede

[30] Several (40 + 21)s appeared as persistent road signs pointing out our destination as a local congregation such as a forty-day corporate fast of our congregation called by the pastor to start on February 21, 1999, and then another forty-day fast within which arrived Israel's Independence Day on April 21, 2000. A national forty-day fast was scheduled to start September 19, 1999, and continue through October 31. This was so significant, as September 19 was the eve of Yom Kippur, and October 31 was the prophetic deadline for repentance for this nation! Our pastor forgot to announce the fast on Sunday the 11th, so he changed the forty-day fast from September 21 to October 30. Not knowing any of this on the night before its start, an intercessor read Isaiah 61 over the pastor. It was a complete 40 + 21 = 61. On November 21, 1999, my husband had a dream that I needed a larger vehicle. We were specifically instructed to go shopping Friday, December 10, and then were led that day to a particular lot, which we had never considered before. It began to rain and there was no business there other than us. We smoothly purchased a used Grand Cherokee with the new tag number M340219. The next morning, as I lay in bed singing silently in my heart to the Lord, He showed me the significance of the new tag. M 3 40 21 9. Three (3) times I had kept a forty-day fast on liquids. (Three times our congregation had also kept a collective forty-day fasts.) Twenty-one (21) is the number for revival (21 Tishri) when rivers of living water flow from within us (John 7:38). Forty (40) + 21 = 61 equates to the miraculous ministry of Christ in Isaiah 61. The nine (9) represents the fullness of the Spirit and harvest. And 61 + 9 = 70, the forerunner spirit with which many identified. The M stood for the new millennium, the twenty-first century just one year and twenty-one days away! It was an SUV: Spirit Utilized Vehicle. Later the Lord called me to buy a new Liberty (50) Jeep on July 4 of 2003 and reclaim the custody of the tag that my son had briefly. I chose the Freedom Series, for many captives will be set free as they are liberated from sin and death. The sunroof declares an open heaven, and black refers to His beautiful black children who will carry the torch in Baltimore just as they did in Los Angeles at the start of the twentieth century.

revival (**21** Tishri), an ongoing habitation of His manifest presence, and culminate in a wide range of the corporate church engaged in the miraculous ministry of Christ (Isaiah **61**) here in the earth before His return. This is manifested union, the same ministry that Jesus proclaimed in the synagogue of Nazareth (Luke 4:18 quoting from Isaiah. **61**:1-2) and then demonstrated through His ministry before the world: preaching good news to the poor, healing the sick, restoring the wounded, and delivering the captives. Both the *voluntary* Teshuvah (**40**) of prolonged fasts *before* 2000 as well as the *involuntary* Teshuvah (**40**) of fiery trials, persecution, judgments, terrorist attacks, wars, and natural disasters after 2000 would precede this glorious end-time revival (**21**). Repetitive Teshuvah will shake the slumbering church awake to be refined as His glorious bride and arise with healing in her wings and heartfelt intercession for the lost, all in God's timing, the acceptable year of the Lord (Isaiah **61**:2). Within this accelerated maturation period there are three reviving seasons which started on the first modern Israel's year of Jubilee.

Isaiah **61** describes the "year of the favor of our Lord" (the sabbatical year of release) and especially the year of Jubilee (**50**), not just in ancient history but in our present day as well. Upon entering the Promised Land in the days of Joshua, the Hebrews were commanded to rest the land every seventh year, calling it a sabbatical year of rest, or release. The year after seven times seven years was called the Jubilee (7 x 7 + 1 = **50**). It was a *new beginning*, or opportunity, for God's people who had lost their land to reclaim their inheritance every **fifty** years. But upon continued sin and spiritual adultery, the vast majority of the Israelites were eventually dispersed throughout the earth.[31] Yet as a covenant-keeping God, Jehovah finally called them back "as a nation" just as He had promised (Lev. 26:33-45). And the Jews

[31] This is the fifth, or final, cycle of discipline outlined in Deuteronomy chapter 28.

reentered their land and became the modern nation of Israel on Friday, May 14, 1948 (5 Iyar 5708), as prophesied by Isaiah. It was a greater new beginning for the Jews to reclaim their natural inheritance.

> **Who hath heard such a thing? who hath seen such things? Shall the earth be made to bring forth in one day? or shall a nation be born at once? for as soon as Zion travailed, she brought forth her children. (Isaiah 66:8)**

Fifty years later was May 14, 1998 (18 Iyar 5758), but officially, Israel's first modern Jubilee started a few months later on the Day of Atonement [Yom Kippur] (Lev. 25:8), on September 30, 1998 (10 Tishri 5759). Normally it would end on Yom Kippur, September 20, 1999 (10 Tishri 5760), but Israel extended theirs to their Independence Day, April **21**, 2000 (5 Iyar 5760), at Pesach or Passover, the early harvest time. That means two early or spring harvests (two Passovers) in one Jubilee! Very unusual. Was there a reason for all this? Oh, yes.

The church always follows Israel. The church's Jubilee (a very special *new beginning*) also began on Yom Kippur, September 30, 1998, but as that date neared, I questioned if this was truly significant, so the Lord provided me this dream:

> **09/24/98: I was in an office being told details about a house, as if by a Realtor. I remember thinking I wasn't interested and it probably didn't have four bedrooms as we have for all four of us, but she said it did. Another person told me that if I got there by 10:30 a.m., I would be given $61. The directions were from the house I was raised in. I was to turn right at the end of 10th Street and go beyond the cemetery where my natural father was buried. I heard "a sure house," which refers to inclusion of family and descendants.**

Upon awaking, I reasoned (function of our soul) that this might have to do with the salvation of my father's household for which I was standing in faith. Just to be on the safe side, I drove to our congregational facility and arrived right before 10:30 a.m., thinking He may ask me to stay sixty-one hours to pray for my father's household. I began reading Lamentations as it was next in line.[32] My heart was heavy for souls for I sensed the 1999 spring harvest (Reinhardt Bonnke's *Beyond '99*) might be missed by the church locally. I had already been weeping when a Master's Commission student, Louis, asked if I would like to hear Robert Stearns' latest *River* CD, at that time called *Lament for the Poor*. I agreed and he put it on. As the music played, the dream's interpretation unfolded.

The first song paraphrased its lyrics from Isaiah **61**: "This is the year of the favor of the Lord."[33] A prophetic word proclaimed that the power would not flow in the streets until compassion flowed there. I wept (lamented) all the more for the Father's house (our congregation, the Baltimore region, and our nation). The directions have come right from the heavenly Father. It is beyond the grave,[34] for it is resurrection power that will gradually increase within the bride after *that* Day of Atonement, **10** Tishri, the end of the Ten (**10**) Days of Awe falling on September **30** by our solar calendar on that particular year. God wants a sure house = many children. The four bedrooms declare there will be room for *all* (north, south, east, and west). So began our year of Jubilee (**50**)! It was a starting point of a special period in which the bride made ready will blossom to full ma-

[32] The Lord had instructed me to read the entire Bible that month to keep *Simchat Torah*. I did not know until years later that this was only done in the year of Jubilee.

[33] Robert Stearns, "Spirit Of The Sovereign God," *The River Vol. 3: Lament for the Poor*, CD Track 1, Eagles Wings, 1998.

[33] My natural father's house was on 10th Street, and his burial site was just beyond it.

turity and harvest a massive multitude of souls as tribute to her Beloved before He returns. Though it started on September 30, 1998, in Hebrew terms it was already 1999. That is important to remember.

The Lord gave me a second confirmation on the eve of Yom Kippur. When I arrived at our church facility that Tuesday evening, September 29, I was impressed to turn on our lighted cross at 6:35 p.m. just as the Jewish candles were being lit. A teenage boy, Shawn, who ran the soundboard, was there with me. He put on a CD and I was caught up with worship when I suddenly remembered the light. I opened my eyes to discover Shawn walking to the cross light switch and turning it on. I sighed deeply thinking the timing had been missed, but when I checked my watch, I discovered that it was exactly 6:35 p.m. This was the start of a new beginning for the church, the whole church worldwide. And the significance of this new beginning is astounding.

There have been two new beginnings for the church connected to the two Israeli harvest seasons (early and latter). The new beginning (**8**) of the early harvest (7 days of Passover + 1 days of Pentecost = **8**) was at Acts 2 for a jumpstart of the newborn church on the fiftieth (**50**) **day** after Passover. But this is a far, far greater new beginning (**8**) of the latter or autumn harvest (7 days of the Feast of Tabernacles + 1 day of Shemini Atzeret = **8**, Lev. 23:34,39 42; Neh. 8:14, 18) linked with the fiftieth (**50**) **year** Jubilee (not day). This is a far, far superior new beginning for the body of Christ to reclaim all our inheritance in Christ including lost souls and our nation! God declares: "For the earth is the Lord's and the fullness thereof and ALL the people that dwell therein" (Ps. 24:1). That is a big promise, but God made it! Nothing is impossible with God! And it is unraveling soon.

The multiplicative difference of fifty *days* in comparison to fifty *years* is overwhelming in magnitude (365 times)! This huge difference symbolizes the differences of the "former rain" moderately (Acts 2) and "former and latter rain" together coming soon! And so will be the escalating enormity of purity and power of the maturing bride in these end-days and the massive harvest of souls she will reap! It will far exceed the mass salvations of the book of Acts. Whole cities and nations will be reaped! It has already begun—a distinct starting point divinely set by God on a distinct *chronos* day in history. And it was a small and unknown beginning, as was the birth of our Lord Jesus in a stable. Yet it will impact the whole world **thirty-three** years later, as did He. And so shall be the impact of the bride of Christ within a similar God-ordained maturation period!

Like Israel, the church's Jubilee started in 1998 (really, 1999, by the Hebrew thought) and was extended into a second spring or early harvest in 2000. Prior to this, during Passover, April 13, 1998 (the day after Easter), several pastors staked the entrances of the city of Baltimore, and a friend of mine took pictures, but they turned out double exposed from her granddaughter's second birthday party. One picture was of the Bishop BP and Pastor TK, staking the East Gate of Baltimore at I-95 on the property of a local congregation. There is a way by which the King is coming and it is through the East Gate—not only in Jerusalem but in cities such as Baltimore and in nations as well! The overlaid picture was of a little girl blowing out two candles on her birthday cake. She was born the day after Easter two years before. This confirmed that our nation's Jubilee would be extended beyond the early harvest of 1999 to the early harvest of 2000, just like Israel's Jubilee.

What is the significance of this? Hundreds of congregations across the USA (at least four in Baltimore) distributed Reinhardt Bonnke's *Beyond '99* booklets in the 1999 early harvest, and thousands of congregations united across the nation (200 in Baltimore) distributed the *Book of Hope* in the 2000 early harvest![35] This has never happened before nor has it happened again, as yet! Interestingly, shortly thereafter the harvest of 2000, Baltimore kept its first Jesus Day rally right on the Hebrew day of Pentecost, Saturday, June 10, with ninety congregations collectively walking simultaneously one of fifty (**50**) one to one and a half mile segments around the city (within I-695) before a united celebration in the city. This feast was kept globally that day and continues to be kept globally, though it has changed titles and coordinating ministries. It was once called Jesus Day, but since 2005 it has been called the Global Day of Prayer (GDOP),[36] which has expanded to every nation, reaching in participation to several hundred million believers around the globe. Whether it continues under this title or not, we must gather together each Pentecost to seek God for the promised greater outpouring of His Spirit promised. During this first reviving season, there was also an ongoing prayer-evangelism movement called the Lighthouse Movement across the nation. One million homes of believers were praying for their neighbors.

The early harvest season has great significance in city-reaching! God charged Joshua and the Israelites to cross the Jordan River to take the city of Jericho when "the Jordan overfloweth all his banks all the time of harvest" (Josh. 3:15b). Rahab had barley on her roof, and that means it was the early harvest, not the latter or fall harvest. The fifty days of Passover to Pentecost are the prescribed time for harvesting cities! But it will require flood-stage glory to actually achieve the desired results. Both in 1999 and 2000 we united, we distributed, but the results in salvations were minuscule. And yet the church thereafter has grown

[35] Cooperative work of CBN and Mission America.

[36] www.gdopusa.com

in sincere fellowship and unity among pastors and ministry leaders meeting and praying together regularly. Community and regional networks were set in place. As we continue this fellowship of unity, we prepare ourselves to collectively flow in manifested union with Christ, for there are at least two more appointed reviving seasons with far greater harvest opportunities yet to come!

I first caught a glimpse of these three reviving seasons at my first visit to TACF[37] in August of 1995. A speaker shared briefly three different prophetic words concerning three separate revivals in the future. The first was around 2000. The second was in the early 2000-teens, and the third one in the early 2000-thirties. All three words had come from different Vineyard churches. Four years later I recognized their association to the life and ministry of Jesus Christ our Beloved as recorded in Scripture: His birth through age two, when He was twelve at the Temple, and His three-plus years of ministry starting at age thirty to **thirty-three**. His greatest accomplishment was on the cross for our salvation at the age of **thirty-three**. So it will be with the end-day bride.

God has been announcing this **thirty-three** year period for some time now and increasingly as it has begun. Foremost, our Lord Jesus lived **thirty-three** years on earth. Jesus came through the line of King David (a type of Christ) who reigned in Jerusalem for **thirty-three** years (2 Sam. 5:4-5). One of DC Comics' super heroes, Superman[38] started his mission at age **thirty-three**. J. R. Tolkien's novel, *Lord of the Rings,* many feel is prophetic and came out as a movie for such a time as this. It is in-

[37] TACF is the Toronto Airport Christian Fellowship in Toronto, Ontario, Canada.

[38] In *Man of Steel,* Jo El was a type of the Father, his name meaning in Hebrew, "Jehovah Mighty." Jo El sent his son, Kal El, a type of Jesus, to earth to live among men. Kal started his mission to save the world when he was thirty-three-years old. God speaks to us in many ways.

teresting that the ring-bearer, Frodo Baggins, was **thirty-three** years old the day he received the ring (his destined part for the king's return). And that **thirty-three** years was the age a hobbit was deemed mature. Though Fordo received the ring on his **thirty-third** birthday, he did not begin his final quest of destiny until his **fiftieth** birthday. William Branham[39] prophesied of two specific **thirty-three**-year periods (1933-1966, 1966-1999) which perfectly line up with this period in which we are presently living (1999-2032). This present **thirty-three**-year period of accelerated maturation began on modern Israel's first Jubilee, or **fiftieth** year. It makes sense that the former life and earthly ministry of Christ should be walked out by the end-day bride of Christ. He is the first and the last. And we are flesh of His flesh and bone of His bone. We are one in spirit and becoming one in soul. So finalizing His work on the earth within a **thirty-three**-year span of time *now* through the end-day bride makes sense, especially when it parallels His life and ministry while He was here on earth. **These three reviving seasons are within a thirty-three-year span of end-time.**

September 30, 1998,[40] (like Israel May 14, 1948) was not just the Jubilee of modern Israel but also the rebirth of the church, another holy nation in a single day throughout the earth. It was a distinct point in chronological time from which the church will mature in ministry over this **thirty-three**-year period in tribute to our Lord. The **first reviving season** (1999, 2000) produced an unnoticeable harvest of souls because the bride was but a newborn in city-reaching and regional and national transformation. And yet, many harvesting ministries and prayer net-

[39] Though I do not agree with all of Branham's teachings, the miracles performed confirm God's favor. He was a *prophetic* man of God. No one has the complete understanding of the Word of God.

[40] By Hebrew thought, it was already 1999.

works were born in the humblest of places, as was our Lord in a stable, with very little attention from the world (secular or religious). And just as in our Lord's infant days, visions and dreams are multiplying and angelic visitations are rising. And often the least distinguished (like the shepherds) will find Him first. And just as the Magi brought the toddler Christ gold, frankincense, and myrrh, *so* have come to His beloved bride gold specks, gold nuggets, the fragrance of true spiritual worship, as well as the myrrh of death to self in fasting and prayer. In some places death is steadily increasing through persecution, genocide, and terrorism reminiscent of Herod's horrific massacre of Bethlehem's male children two and under. But somewhere before 2032, the church will begin to *truly* leave her sojourn in Egypt (the world) just as did our Lord (Matt. 2:19-22) by prophetic rhema and dreams. And the bride will become the "separated one" (Matt. 2:23 Amplified Version) sheltered often in remote places of little promise in man's sight, like Nazareth.

As of the early 2000-teens, the church has entered the **second reviving season.** The bride of Christ will increase in wisdom and in stature and in favor with God and mankind throughout the earth (Luke 2:52). She will be stronger in spirit, filled with wisdom and grace, and walk in His favor and blessing (Luke 2:40), for as it was with Jesus so will it be with His bride in every arena of business, politics, research, education, etc. Not all the church will be perfectly on time, however. There will always be some individual Christians, congregations, networks, and even nations that are on the forefront heralding the next level of maturity; some will linger well behind. But within the second reviving season, we will reach great proportions of revival as we mature more and more in Christ character and in works. Many places will be transformed. Then, in about the early 2030s, a fully matured, holy, spotless bride, after much fiery refinement (Teshuvah) as our Lord experienced in the wilderness (Luke

4:1-14), will walk in the full miracle-working power of God as exemplified by the firstborn of many brethren, our Groom and Head, the Lord Jesus Christ the Righteous! (Luke 4:18). And a global harvest of inconceivable number will follow her as she follows Christ. **This third reviving season will perfectly mirror our Lord's ministry on earth.**

Each is an appointed *season* of Almighty God that we dare not miss before our Lord's return. And every harvest opportunity within them will exponentially increase with the maturing of the bride in character and unity. When the word of God increases, the number of disciples multiplies (Acts 6:7). To increase and to multiply are two totally different things. Adding ten to ten is no comparison to multiplying ten by ten. When the Word increases, the harvest *multiplies.* What is this "Word?" It is the Greek *logos.* Logos means the "full embodiment of the Word of God." Jesus was and is *the* Word, "the Logos made flesh" (John 1:1, 14). This Word that multiplies, Logos, will more and more manifest through the emerging holy bride in nature and in deed. *He* is increasing, i.e., arising within His bride as she matures. From infant stage, to seemingly youthful teens, and then finally, to a fully mature, thirty-plus bride who will walk in her destined glory of the Lord. And with each level of increased maturity, there will be a much greater *multiplied* harvest that we might reclaim *all* our inheritance in Christ! Personally, I had my heart totally fixed on the third season in the 2030s, and almost missed sharing what could be the present day church's last season. Thank God that He is loving and kind and that His mercy endures forever, for we desperately need it to recognize our corporate place and fulfill our corporate calling.

The second reviving season is upon us *now.* It is time to prepare and watch over this present-day harvest of family, neighbors, friends, and co-workers. And this season could be the church's last opportunity to reach the lost collectively across this nation and others. On the tenth day of 2010's Ten Days of Prayer (Saturday, May 22, 2010) preceding the Global Day of Prayer (Pentecost Sunday, May 23, 2010), the Lord spoke this thought into my mind while in prayer. "What if the third [reviving][41] season is to be fulfilled by the 144,000 Jewish missionaries of Revelation 7? What if this second [reviving] season is the last opportunity for the present-day church?" I was profoundly stunned and could not speak for quite some time. I felt disappointed, for I long for the miraculous! I had set my heart on the third reviving season at the expense of not trumpeting the second. The weight and disappointment seemed enormous! With sadness I inquired if there might be any signs and wonders and miracles in the second season.

The Holy Spirit immediately reassured and reminded me that before any miracle had been recorded in our Lord's ministry, Mary, His mother, already knew something was very special about her son, Jesus. She had observed Him growing up. That is why she told the servants at the marriage in Cana, "Do whatever He tells you to do." Mary knew that if they did what He said, it would happen, even if it required a miracle, like turning water into wine. Yes, there will be miracles—an ocean of miracles! All the bride must do is hear and obey and do it His way using the Word of knowledge and other gifts of the Spirit poured out upon her. I also questioned the Lord about this season linked to Jesus' experience at the Temple in Jerusalem at age twelve and beyond. Age twelve in Western cultures is but a child, but in biblical days the age of twelve was the passage from boyhood to

[41] The Lord actually said, "three harvest seasons." But while writing this book, I felt this phrase of "harvest seasons" could be mixed up with reference to Israel's yearly early and latter harvest seasons (Pentecost and Feast of Tabernacles), so I changed what the Lord said to "three (reviving) seasons," and that is why the word "reviving" is in parenthesis here. It was not His spoken word.

manhood, or maturity! In the sight of God, the church's unity will mature enough for the task of taking cities and nations for Christ in this second reviving season!

The Lord confirmed this word the next day via national TV. After returning home from the Global Day of Prayer gathering in Harford County, Maryland, I decided to relax and watch something on one of the Hallmark channels. Suddenly, I had a burden for lost souls. With sobs, I cried out to God for the lost. Strangely, the burden quickly lifted off me, and I turned to Channel 2, which I normally don't watch. It was 7 p.m. and they were starting a review of the TV series called *Lost* before airing the last episode of its last season. I watched for a while and then reasoned (a function of the soul) that this was ridiculous. Though I knew this was a popular series, I had never watched it before. After about an hour I turned back to Hallmark until 9 p.m. But I knew (a function of the spirit) that I had to watch it. So I switched back to Channel 2 and as soon as I did, the glory of God came so heavily upon me that I could not move until it was over at 11:30 p.m. God did not speak to me through the script but through the event: **the last season for the Lost**. He was confirming to me that this second reviving season beginning in the early 2000-teens is indeed the last opportunity for the present-day church to collectively harvest cities and nations![42] We don't have much time, and we must do this *together*!

We have just entered the second reviving season. Originally I assumed by simple math[43] that it would start somewhere within 2010 to 2012. But it did not. It started exactly as foretold

[42] Some communities are already doing it. Check out missionamerica.org for some examples.

[43] Jesus' age of twelve added to 1998-2000 would be 2010-2012. That was my original assumption of the start of the second reviving season, but many prophetic believers sensed those years were merely transitional years. They were correct.

by the Vineyard prophecy—the early teens (2013-2014). How do I know? There were no signs between 2010 and 2012.[44] In early 2013, I asked the Lord once again if 2013 and 2014 were truly the starting point of this second reviving season. My eyes immediately went to two paintings called the *Sonnet Twins* by the Persian artist Arbe. My husband and I (pair of two) purchased them while celebrating our twenty-fifth wedding anniversary on a cruise. I always knew there were only twenty-five pairs of these two paintings throughout the world but I had never examined their individual copy numbers. That moment I checked. They are number thirteen and number fourteen. That was enough for me. This second reviving season is upon us *now* and will continue possibly to 2029. We may have a few years more or less. No one knows but the Father. Interestingly, the same prayer-evangelism movement of the first reviving season has reignited under a new name: LOVE2020. Its goal is for every street in the United States of America to be covered by at least one believer with prayer, care, and share by the year 2020.[45] It is a 2020 vision, the perfect eyesight of God for this nation.

Every community or city (Ps. 24:1) belongs to Christ and His bride. Specifically, I know Baltimore does. How? Because He said it and He always keeps His word. Let me explain. In 2010, while reading about the life and ministry of a deceased healing evangelist, the Lord kindled my faith in some Scriptures he often used. Remember, Jesus came to earth stripped of His power as deity; He laid it aside and took on flesh to dwell among us (Phil. 2). That is why He said, "The Son can do nothing of himself, but what he seeth the Father do" (John 5:19). And He said,

[45] www.LOVE2020.com

[44] I saw numbers in the sky two days after He spoke of this last season for the church. I saw: 88, 99, 00, 11, and 22 referring to 1988, 1999, 2000, 2011, 2022. At first I thought this was for all the church and shared this information, but I now understand it was personal. I apologize for that.

"I speak to the world those things which I have heard of him" (John 8:26). Jesus could do nothing miraculous as a human being except what He *saw* His Father do or *heard* His Father say. When the Father revealed some act to Him visually (by vision), Jesus obediently *did it* with miraculous results. When the Father spoke to Him, Jesus obeyed and *said it* with miraculous results. It was already done when it was shown or told to Him, for it was the will of the Father. Jesus came to do the will of His Father. And the Father's will has not changed.

Likewise, *without* Christ we can do nothing (John 15:5b) but with Christ all things are possible (Matt.19:26) *in* and *for* and *through* us. The Holy Spirit reminded me of past experiences demonstrating His ministry method of the Word of knowledge. One time, as I was talking with an intercessor friend, I kept seeing myself place my index fingers in her ears. I saw it several times until I finally told her. She eagerly asked me to pray as she had had ear problems for months. I put my fingers in her ears and she was healed. It was easy. I just did what Christ in me was showing me to do, and the Lord healed her. Another time, I was talking with a young neighbor mother with her ill toddler dangling listlessly in her arms. He had a high fever. I kept seeing myself lay my right hand on his head. Inside, I argued with God that she may not be saved while outwardly talking with her. Finally, as I was leaving, I tapped his head and said, "Be healed." He was, instantly! All because it was the will of God and He showed me His will so He could accomplish His will through me. That is how the Lord wills to work through His church. Once, an unsaved neighbor called me on my cell phone while she was in extreme pain from a spinal injury and out of my mouth came, "As soon as I get home, I will be right over to pray for you." I did not intend on making that statement, but He did (Matt. 10:20). Christ in me said it. He healed her when I obeyed and she received Christ shortly thereafter. He brought all this to my remembrance. So we can be confident, even for the city of Baltimore.

Baltimore will be saved because I already *saw* it and *heard* Him say it! Let me share further. In 1991 I had my first burden for Baltimore. I went into a vision of hundreds of thousands of people in utter darkness moving forward without any knowledge of where they were going. Finally, they reached the edge of a great cliff, and in terror, they fell into hell one row after another. It was an agonizing scene to witness, and it stayed with me for three years, always thrusting me into deep intercession. Finally in 1994 I *saw* a great golden net (network of the church) catch the people and I *heard* the Lord say, "Seven hundred thousand." This number represents Baltimore. It was confirmed to me by a Peruvian missionary and a book written about Baltimore in 1905, which on page 53,[46] mentioned the city's population then of seven hundred thousand. I saw it and I heard it. It is finished in Christ! He has given the unified church of Baltimore the city of Baltimore. She only has to possess it together!

We may not see all seven hundred thousand saved in this second season, for the third season will claim far, far more. Yet I sense that it will only require a Gideon army to take whole regions. But the necessary seed of God's Word must be sown into their hearts soon so they will come to Christ in this season or in the third. And the water of the Word must be continually applied for the maturation of those that are saved in this second season and beyond. More than ever, the bride of Christ must increase her love[47] for one another and faithfully support Jehovah's beloved Israel. It will be our awakened Jewish brothers and sisters that will lead the third reviving season harvesting

[46] As in Isaiah 53.

[47] www.LOVE2020.com

our loved ones, friends, and neighbors still in darkness after our rapture departure.

The bride faithful must prayerfully prepare the way for these 144,000 Jewish missionaries to whom the Gospel baton will be passed in this great race for mankind.

> **And I heard the number of them which were sealed: *and there were* sealed an hundred and forty and four thousand of all the tribes of the children of Israel. (Rev. 7:4)**

That is twelve thousand of each of the twelve tribes of Israel. God called the nation of Israel to spread the Word of His glory throughout the earth since Abraham and Moses, but over the centuries, most went after false gods and religious works. But "the gifts and callings of God are without repentance" (Rom. 11:29). They are irrevocable. God has not changed His mind. He is a covenant-keeping God, and He is not finished with the Jews. There has always been a faithful remnant even today. They are presently born again in Christ and will leave in the rapture with the rest of the present-day bride of Christ. Of those Jews remaining, 144,000 will suddenly recognize Jesus as their Messiah, having been made jealous of our end-day glory walk with God. The apostle Paul explained that Israel's blindness to salvation was permitted for our sake to allow the reconciliation of the Gentiles to Christ to come to its full number. But when we leave, this new remnant will awaken as the mighty torchbearers of the Gospel amid the darkest days of tribulation (Rom. 11:15, 25). They will walk in the full manifestation of Christ, as did our Lord while on earth! Let's keep the feasts, win the lost, and give seed to the Jews to help awaken them at our leave.

CHAPTER 9

LIVING JUBILEE IN TESHUVAH

The bride made ready will live in Jubilee even while involuntary Teshuvah escalates throughout the earth. At the start of our nation's first reviving season (1999, 2000), during the years of modern Israel's first Jubilee, I sensed great Teshuvah would begin. The Lord confirmed this to me through a life experience. In November of 1998, I was unknowingly driving to my prayer site above the speed limit (doing **51**[48] mph in a 35 mph zone), and I was caught. After prayer that morning, I returned to my vehicle to go home. The Lord said to me, "Judgment will begin at **fifty-one,**" meaning the year after our Jubilee: in other words, 2001. The fine for my speeding was $70. Biblically, "seventy" means "forerunner," but it also means "prior to increase." So judgment would begin and continue to increase from the year 2001. Just as the church's Jubilee is not confined to one chrono-

[48] In August 2010 the address of the mosque willed by Muslims to be built near Ground Zero was Park **51** i.e., "park" or "stay" claiming the land where terror happened. The devil builds strongholds by trauma. As though this was known, I heard that there was planned **fifty-one** continuous hours of worship and intercession for DC. On August 23, 2011, I was writing about the significance of this **fifty-one** days (October 3, 2011, through November 22, 2011), which covered the Ten Days of Awe and the Feast of Tabernacles, when my house shook and I looked at the clock. It was an earthquake, and it happened at 1:**51** p.m., which was later confirmed by Fox News.

logical year, so is it also with judgments[49] in the earth. Both the church's Jubilee (1998-2000) and judgment (2001 and beyond) were starting points from which the bride will continue to arise to shine and our adversary to arise to fall. For my traffic ticket, I was instructed to go to court, admit my guilt, and ask for the mercy of the court. The judge did not cancel the $70 fine, but he did cancel the points on my driver's license, which (through increased insurance rates) could have cost a total of seven times the fine over the next few years. No amount of intercession will stop judgment on the United States, but crying out for mercy will greatly confine the extent of judgment! We must cry out for mercy! We must plead the blood of Jesus, for unlike Abel's blood and all other innocent bloodshed, Jesus' blood cries for mercy!

The world witnessed the beginning of our nation's end-day judgments on September **11**, 2001, when the two World Trade Center buildings and the Pentagon were viciously attacked and thousands of precious lives lost in an utterly senseless act of unprecedented terrorism. Why America, the nation foremost in sharing the Gospel? He chastens whom He loves. An email shared all the "**elevens**" of that day.[50] The number "**eleven**" conveys judgment (**11**) but is also defined as "incompleteness; disorganization; disintegration." It is beyond ten (natural law and government) and short of twelve (divine government, apostolic fullness).[51] Terrorist attacks are outside the bounds of all law and

49 The word "judgment" is also translated "justice." Judgment of one may bring justice to another.

50 "The date of attack: 9/**11** - 9+1+1=**11**. September 11th is the 254th day of the year: 2+5+4=**11**. After September **11**th there are 111 days left to the end of the year. 119 is the area code to Iraq/Iran. Twin Towers standing side by side looks like the number **11**. The first plane to hit the towers was Flight **11**. State of New York—the **11**th state added to the Union. New York City - **11** letters. Afghanistan - **11** letters. The Pentagon - **11** letters. Flight **11** - 92 on board - 9+2=**11**. Flight 77 had 65 on board - 6+5=**11**. And dial 9-1-1 for an emergency."

51 Kevin J. Conner, *Interpreting the Symbols and Types* (Portland, Oregon: Bible Temple Publications, 1980), 7.

orderly government, however Islamic terrorists well depict the prophecy of the ten toes of intermixed iron and clay in Nebuchadnezzar's dream (Dan. 2:42). It is a *decentralized* (**11**) empire in pieces throughout the earth.[52] It lacks central top-down organization in many regions; it has *incomplete* (**11**) communications and coordination; and it will *disintegrate* (**11**) with time from within as all evil does (Dan. 2:44). But for now the terrorists of Islam and other terrorist groups are God's agent for our good, for it takes great Teshuvah to shake up the slumbering church to assess her walk, her motives, her priorities, and get down to seeking His face, fleeing from sin, and beginning to reap the harvest.

As we approach the opportunities during the second reviving season, we are beginning to more readily distinguish the tares from the wheat. The tares (including terrorists) are growing right alongside the wheat, and they are actually instrumental in *our* maturation. Natural havoc and terrorist activity not only prepare *us* for the harvest, it slaps those lost in sin into recognizing the dire state of their lives and their need for a Savior! This is a necessary component, for in peace and prosperity, the church of the United States obtained very little results from the 1999 and 2000 harvest opportunities. But hereafter, the judgments and other forms of Teshuvah will initiate far greater harvests all in His perfect timing. And those most prepared will reap the greater harvest portions.

Our 911 was a national Teshuvah, or judgment (**11**) God *permitted* for our good[53] and for the sake of harvest (**9**). Many souls were shaken and saved as an outcome, but there is much more

[52] Hamas, al-Queda, ISIS, Boko Haram, al-Nusra. al-Sharia, Hezbollah, the Muslim Brotherhood, al-Murabitun, and the list goes on.

[53] There is revival in this 09/**11**/01: 9 + **11** + 1 = 21.

yet to transpire as a result. On August 26, 2002,[54] a group of prayer leaders went to Ground Zero to pray. As we approached the site, I was drawn to the building across from Ground Zero. It was the Century **21** building. As we left the site, I was drawn to the particular intersection of the streets Church and Liberty (**50**). Then we walked to the Ground Zero Prayer Center at the intersection of John and 11th Streets (**11**). The founders had recognized this as "John chapter 11," the resurrection of Lazarus. Ultimately, all mankind will be judged (**11**) and resurrected (**11**) unto eternal life or death. But before that day, God is reviving the end-day church on earth! She will be liberated, authorized, and empowered in this **twenty-first** century to fulfill her call, the Great Commission, while walking in the Great Commandment! And because Century **21** is a realty company, God is declaring that He is willing to redeem our land as well!

Judgment (**11**) is necessary for the sake of the harvest (**9**) and fullness of God's character (**9**) and gifts (**9**) within our lives to rightfully reap the souls of men. Throughout Scripture God used a rod (specifically, a *mattah*) in the hand of His prophets or leaders to spread out or to smite the ground in judgment or correction. God used Moses' rod to "smite their enemies," saying, "I [Jehovah] will smite the waters" (Exod. 7:14-20) etc. This smite is in the permissive state. God does not smite people, but where there is sin, He must permit the consequences of unrepentant sin—especially corporate sin—to manifest. Through Moses, Jehovah God smote, or judged, Egypt with plagues.

The mattah was and still is used (at the direction of the Lord of hosts) to besiege or take cities in spiritual warfare as we smite or pierce through spiritual darkness, not people. The *enemies* of God are judged, and cities are redeemed from curses. Also

[54] While at the Citywide Prayer Leaders Consultation in the Empire State Building, King's College, New York, NY.

these rods were used scripturally for chastening, for He chastens those whom He loves, His children. The word "smite" means "to strike for the sake of correction." God warned Israel that if they disobeyed His Word or commands, He would (permit them to be smitten) with a curse in Deuteronomy 28:22, 27, 28, and 35. *His Word is His rod.* Often, when Israel departed from God, He would (permissively) smite them through attacks by their enemies, which would then lead them to repentance. Once more, His blessings would be poured out upon them. Due to sin in our land, God permitted the smiting of America twice (the Twin Towers) with the rod of the World Trade Center. He used the church's enemy (the most vile tares, the terrorists of Islam) to chasten us unto repentance. Pride and independence fell that day, and humility and dependency upon God rose from the ashes for a season, for God gives grace to the humble. But has pride crept back? We must keep on guard.

Amazingly, these most extreme tares, the terrorists, imitate the same growth pattern as the most fervent wheat. One of the details the Lord spoke of concerning the end-day revival is that it would be *homegrown and not imported.* Before the **twenty-first** century in Baltimore, our congregation and clusters of congregations often kept the feasts with outside speakers coming to us, but God said that revival would come from within the home body and city. It would be planted locally with prophetic words, watered with intercession and tears, and reaped by those who have labored within its field. The wheat is maturing to reap an ongoing revival (**21**) and spiritual liberty (**50**) for a massive harvest of souls in the character (**9**) and power of Christ (**9**). But the tares are also maturing to reap judgments (**11**) upon themselves [in Teshuvah (**40**) toward us], judgments of fear, death, and eternal damnation in the nature of Satan. Both wheat and tares are maturing together.

Consider God's message to us from August **9**, 2006.[55] The evil plans unveiled were a type of **9** Av[56] for the United States. The initial reports on the Internet on August 10[57] (though those numbers would change over the next few days) were: **fifty** suspected as being involved, **twenty-one** arrested, **nine** planes targeted, and that the plot was homegrown by British Muslims. Two days later there were **forty** picked up for questioning in Italy.[58] The tares are growing alongside the wheat. The church's liberty (**50**), revival (**21**), harvest (**9**), and Teshuvah (**40**) are being countered by the movement of death and darkness. God is also conveying to us that the impact of these extremists parallels the extent of our own potential impact though small Christian prayer groups and congregations. Just as it does not require a great number of terrorists (if successful) to impact a large segment of humanity, it will not require many radical lovers of Christ to fan extensive flames of revival.

In this time of Jubilee in Teshuvah, Satan is releasing evil terrorists against Israel and the church, but God is also releasing glory terrorists for the advancement of His Kingdom. And since the Greater One lives in us, we will succeed them. On the first day of Sukkot, the Feast of Tabernacles on October 7, 2006, I was watching a movie that night about a professional assassin who returned to his ten-year high school reunion and the girl

55 I had wondered why all July and early August I had looked at the **9**th of August approaching as though it was the Hebrew **9**th of Av.

56 **9** Av, or **9**th day of the month Av in the Hebrew calendar, is the culminating day of twenty-one days of mourning from Tammuz 17 when the Romans breached the walls of Jerusalem on **9** Av. The first temple was destroyed by the Babylonians and the second temple by the Romans on this exact same day. On this particular Tammuz 17, Hezbollah began the war with Israel and it continued beyond the days of mourning. This is a mourning our Lord will turn to joy!

57 Danica Kirka, "Terrorists Aimed to Blow Up 10 Planes, Some Suspects Still Being Hunted," Associated Press, August 10, 2006, http://www.nysun.com/foreign/terrorists-aimed-to-blow-up-10-planes-/37705/.

58 As reported by Sheila MacVicar on CBS News on August 12, 2006.

he left behind. While back in his hometown, an evil man attempted to take his life and he was forced to kill him in self-defense. She witnessed the body and wanted no part of him until a contract was out on her own father and several professional assassins came to take his life. This one assassin rescued her and her father and took them to the father's house. He told the father and daughter (whom he loved) to hide in the upstairs bathroom. He killed all the assassins and then came into the bathroom covered in blood asking her if she would marry him. The father replied, "You have my blessing." Amazingly, the Spirit of God rose up within me, and I began to laugh. My mind pondered how this could be so funny to me, but I kept laughing and laughing. Moments later, this word came for all who are His bride in preparation.

> **10/07/06: A glory terrorist impacts many lives suddenly, explosively, enduringly, eternally. An explosion of light tears down the barriers of darkness that holds the unsaved in bondage to sin and death. It is an eternal way of escape through the blood of Jesus. The marks of terror were on the cross of Christ. His suffering paid for the liberty of the lost. But the great assassin** [Satan] **will arise with evil in his eyes. He lurks in the despair of men and the agony of their destruction. His promises are false, empty, and deceiving. His depravity is spreading across the nations. His hate is contaminating the hearts of men to a level of evil unimaginable. But I will arise with life! I will arise in My people. I will set off explosions of glory throughout the earth starting in the darkest areas, like the streets of Baltimore.**

He is calling the bride to be glory terrorists for Christ, saying:

> **Will you agree with Me? Will you intercede with Me? Will you stand with Me? Not just desire it, but do it? . . . I will appear in glory and power. I will arise with**

> **healing in My wings. If you will meet Me, I will come in power. If you will lay down your life, I will seed the field of** [any city or community] **and the harvest of souls will come . . . I will make you ready. You can't make yourself ready without My intervention and participation.** [He continued with these specific instructions.] **Get explosive in praise. Get explosive in prayer. Arm yourself with My promises. Keep My Word within your heart . . . Devour it like a starved child. Feed on it continually that I may build you into a mighty warrior in My Spirit, that My sword flash like lightening from your mouth to clash with the dark powers I have already defeated them at the cross. Enough pleasure. Get real. This is a real battle with very high stakes—the souls of hundreds of thousands of people. . . .**

Will you be a glory terrorist for Christ? If so, you must be made ready, and only you and the Lord together can do that.

The impact of a few evil terrorists can be widespread, but they are only the counterfeit of glory terrorists who, few in number, can set whole cities and regions ablaze for Christ. There will be multi-Spirit-coordinated attacks by glory terrorists. These holy fire-filled saints within a given community or region will covertly slip into God-designated sites to set off glory explosions and then slip out, generally without notice. How? Illegally? No; it will be legal. They will assemble for prayer as led by the Spirit of God or be invited to speak into un-anticipating congregations and united gatherings. While there, they will suddenly release volatile explosive words and sounds from the Most High God within, starting unquenchable blazes in seeking dry hearts, and then seemingly vanish. The long-term extent of the work accomplished by God through them could be almost completely undetected at the time. They themselves may not even realize the work done, for most of these fire starters will humbly come from stables, not palaces. But the kindled few of those visited will leaven the entire lump with time. And His fire will spread from heart to heart, congregation to congregation, until whole cities are engulfed in its flames! It only takes a passionate few *homegrown* fire-of-God-carriers to arouse a widespread fervor for revival throughout a given area. As the Master Mind of all time, the Lord of hosts will coordinate these glory attacks simultaneously in multiple cities throughout nations, whether those carrying the torch are known or unknown by other torch-bearers. And no person will be clearly defined as setting the fire ablaze but God, just as those most credited by the acts of terrorists are their unseen leaders. Holy terrorists and unholy terrorists will both work (wheat and tares) to increase God's most brilliant light and night's deepest darkness in the earth before the world is reaped.

Ultimately, our Groom of love is empowering the matured church (His bride made ready) to unite; that we might pray as one, repent as one, praise as one, worship as one, and ultimately, evangelize as one[59] to reap the harvest of all ages. Remember, this book began with 2 Chronicles 16:9 in which God promised to "show Himself strong in behalf of them whose heart is perfect toward Him." The word "behalf" is the Hebrew *im* which means "conjunction" or "communion." (There is "union" in communion.) It comes from the Hebrew *amam*, meaning to "overshadow by huddling" or "gathering together." When together our passion joins His passion, His power shall be fully displayed in our unity. That is keeping the feasts together as He commanded! In so doing, His love in us will abound toward *Him* and *one another* until our consolidated light shines truly bright! The light of the end-day bride will be so brilliant that *all* in darkness will clearly *see* the source of the light. The prodigals

[59] www.LOVE2020.com

and wayward will clearly *see* their way back to Christ. The lost will clearly *see* the repulsiveness of their sin and seek the Savior. The world will clearly *see* the poverty of position and possession and turn to the Crucified Lamb who is now the Risen Lord of all.

But those utterly dark (who have no desire nor ever will have any desire for God) will run deeper into the chasms of death and darkness. And those dimly shining in the church, the five foolish virgins, will either return to the light or recede to "the predicted great falling away of those who have professed to be Christians" (2 Thess. 2:3, AMP). I pray that even there, our merciful Savior will use their fall to violently shake them awake to return to their first love. Overall, light will gravitate to light, and darkness will merge with darkness, so that a line is clearly drawn and the wheat and tares easily discerned. Those still clinging to death and self (the tares) will embrace it and be cut off from Almighty God for eternity. They will be reaped unto damnation. But the wheat, the matured holy, spotless bride will shine in the resplendent beauty of holiness with multitudes of new converts in her wings at the return of the Lord of glory! And she shall sit down at the right side of the King of kings and Lord of lords, the Prince of Peace, the omnipotent One for all eternity in heavenly bliss! For she is His and He is hers, and they are forever one! We will live and even thrive through much Teshuvah when we also live and breathe and have our being in our rightful place of Jubilee.

Again, the first modern Jubilee year of Israel [September 30, 1998 (1999 in Hebrew terms), through May 21, 2000] was merely a starting point for the church. Our spiritual Jubilee will not diminish until God is done, but rather steadily grow in magnitude until the church is removed and the 144,000 Jewish missionaries are sent into the fields by the Lord of the harvest.

We, as the bride made ready, must stay in Jubilee until that time. Our proper anticipation and cooperation are veiled within the definition of the natural Jubilee.

> **And ye shall hallow the fiftieth year, and proclaim liberty throughout *all* the land unto all the inhabitants thereof: it shall be a jubile[60] unto you; and ye shall return every man unto his possession, and ye shall return every man unto his family. (Lev. 25:10)**

Very briefly, the Jubilee was a year to be hallowed, or set apart for God's purposes. It was a year to proclaim liberty to the captives and to all. It was a year for every man to return to his rightful heritage of covenant rights with Yahweh, especially the Promised Land, which, for us, is abundant life in Christ (John 10:10). And it was a year for wayward sons and daughters and spouses to come home.

Should we pursue God in these three reviving seasons (the **thirty-three**-year span of accelerated maturation), God's definition of Jubilee will steadily and increasingly emerge in our lives and in the lives of those we touch.

> **A jubile shall that fiftieth year be unto you: ye shall not sow, neither reap that which groweth of itself in it, nor gather *the grapes* in it of thy vine undressed. (Lev. 25:11)**

The Israelites were not to sow or reap in the sabbatical years (Lev. 25:3-7) or Jubilee. God had promised to exceptionally bless the sixth-year harvest to cover the sabbatical year of rest (every seven years) and the forty-ninth year harvest to provide for the three-year rest period in the Jubilee (Lev. 25:21). In our Jubilee, God has called us to cease from our own agendas to

60 Jubilee in the KJV is spelled "jubile."

pursue His. We are not to be entangled with the world's system and our own pursuits, programs, and plans in these last days, but rather totally seeking the purposes of God while resting in His provision. Even the harvest of souls will come by His Holy Spirit strategies, not ours.

The liberty (**50**) we will attain will transform our whole being of spirit, soul, and body (Isaiah **61**:1-3) for the year of release includes the deliverance of the captives from sin (*spirit* salvation); the recovering of sight to the blind (*physical* salvation, or healing); and liberty to them that were bruised or wounded (*soul* salvation, or restoration). It is also liberty (**50**) for our spouses, our sons, and our daughters captive to drugs, pornography, generational curses, and the worldly spirit. It is the miraculous saving, restoring, healing season God will do *to* His church and then *through* His bride made ready for the believers still slumbering and straddling the fence with the world and the lost still wandering aimlessly in sin and darkness. Liberty is the theme of Jubilee, for we are in Christ, the Master Liberator, and He is in us.

Debts will be canceled, possessions will be restored (Deut. 15:1-3) and blessings will arise and overtake losses, lack, and leanness.

> **In the year of this jubile ye shall return every man unto his possession. (Lev. 25:13)**

A few months after the start of Israel's first modern Jubilee, the nation of Israel received **eleven** billion[61] dollars returned to them via Swiss banks and insurance companies for holocaust victims! The Jubilee is real! James foretold that the rich men "have heaped treasure together for the last days" (James 5:1-3)

[61] Here is an example of "eleven" referring to justice.

for us, the bride, to finance the Gospel worldwide. Argentine evangelists are discovering gold nuggets in their pockets, and they are using it to spread the Gospel. The riches of the wicked are laid up for the just but for His purposes. God "giveth us power to get wealth, that he may establish his covenant" (Deut. 8:18) in the earth, not fund personal carnal desires. In these difficult economic times, we must cleave to the One who loves us, obey His voice, and trust in His provision. He will keep us.

The Jubilee is also the time to demonstrate mercy and compassion on the poor (Deut. 15:7-11).

> **Ye shall not therefore oppress one another; but thou shalt fear thy God: for I *am* the LORD your God. (Lev. 25:17)**

Jesus' half-brother James had a revelation of the end-days. He defined the law of liberty (**50**), or Jubilee, in terms of liberal giving to the poor and needy. James said that walking by faith includes giving to the poor when encountered by their need. We have recently witnessed great generosity within the body of Christ for the tsunami victims in Indonesia, the Katrina victims in Louisiana, the earthquake victims of Haiti, and the super-storm victims of New Jersey and New York. Huge charity organizations have formed to take down malaria, tuberculosis, AIDS, and now, Ebola in Western Africa. These are signs of the times. This is faith in action. Mercy triumphs over judgment, but only those who sow mercy will reap it. The first century church joyfully gave sacrificially to aid others in need (Acts 4:34; 2 Cor. 8:2) *after* first giving *themselves totally to* the Lord. In Matt. 19:21, Jesus says, "If thou wilt be perfect (complete and mature), go and sell that thou hast and give to the poor." The meaning of "hast" here is very specific and refers to the excess we have beyond our needs. It does not mean we become impoverished ourselves but that we do not squander our earnings on excessive things well beyond our necessity. This discipline will readily open the way for us to assist the poor.

The sabbatical year and Jubilee were also times when the Word of God was given due place. All other years, a portion of Torah (specifically the first five books of Moses) was read during the Feast of Tabernacles, but in the year of release, the whole law was read (Deut. 31:9-13). In Nehemiah's day, they remained to hear the Word until 24 Tishri (Neh. 8:18, 9:1-3). It was from this practice of reading Torah that *Simhath Torah* (23 Tishri) was added in modern times. It is called "the rejoicing in Torah" or "Torah of Joy." James 2:12 in the Jewish New Testament says that "Torah which gives freedom" or liberty (**50**). Remember, Torah means "revelation for the purpose of sanctification." There will be revelation released in our season of maturation that will far exceed previous generations, and it will set us apart more and more from the world.

But this **thirty-three**-year period also demands the rightful inclusion of the Word of God once again within our schools and curriculums, businesses, institutions, and government. We *must* declare His sovereign leadership back into all these realms of our nation and seriously proclaim the good news of the Gospel of Jesus Christ to those around us. Like Queen Esther, we must proclaim His Kingdom come and His will be done on earth as it is in heaven until it is. We proclaim His Word; He performs His Word. And this is not just occasionally but consistently within 24/7/365 houses of prayer—home and church altars and corporate and government offices throughout this nation—until His glory flows out into hearts and homes of our loved ones, the drug-infested streets and vile alleys, the shady casinos and debilitating slums, and the oblivious country clubs and hard hearts. Nothing is impossible with Christ *in* us and *through* us!

Finally, within our Jubilee time frame comes the adorning of the bride, which Isaiah prophesied is for the sake of the harvest. "He hath clothed me . . . as a bride adorneth herself with her jewels" (Isaiah **61**:10). His bride is covered with jewels. These are jewels of His character, the shining forth of the fruit (**9**) of His Spirit (Gal. 5:22-25) as well as the supernatural gifts (**9**) of the Spirit in ministry (1 Cor. 12:1-11). These bridal endowments are intended to draw the multitudes of lost souls to Him in and through us. We are to anticipate and expect this covering by faith! These are the final preparations to liberate and empower the end-day bride to reap a harvest of unfathomable enormity, for she will be enwrapped with continual signs, wonders, and miracles!

Why is this important now? Because Jesus is coming very soon for His bride! Its timing is in and through all the Feasts of the Lord. It is through our Jubilee in Teshuvah that He is preparing our hearts to be properly fit for His return! We cannot do it alone, and He will not force in upon us. We must consciously and attentively yield to His preparatory work in us individually and collectively. This is not an option but an indispensable obligation. Like the five wise virgins (Matt. 25:1-10), Luke also records that we are to stay full of His Spirit to keep our "lamps burning like men that wait for their Lord so that when He returns . . . we may open to Him immediately." And He promises to bless His watchful servants (Luke 12:35-37). But He also said that those "who knew his master's will but did not get ready or act as he would wish him to act" will be disciplined as written in verse 47 of the Amplified Bible. The "ready" of this verse is the same Greek word *hetimazo* as the "ready" of Revelation 19:7 for the marriage of the Lamb.

Collectively, the bride made ready will bestow upon her Lord and King a grand and fit reception for His return. Collectively, we will prepare the way of the Lord before His face increasingly as did through John the Baptist (Luke 1:76), then the 12 (Luke 9), then the 70 (Luke 10) and the 120 (Acts 2). Yet in these final days, the latter church, awakened and united, will go before His face in a far, far greater scale then the early church: transforming communities, regions, and even nations. How? First, keeping the feasts individually in lifestyle, loving God and one another etc., as revealed in this book. Second, remembering the Passover kept by Jesus for us. And third, collectively fulfilling the final feast of the church—our final Pentecost. This requires that congregations within given communities gather together to praise, worship, and pray before God annually on that particular feast day.[62] By faith, we are collectively awaiting for the greater outpouring of God's Spirit (Joel 2:23b, 38). Including Holy Communion (our Passover) on Pentecost is a magnificent step toward corporate unity. Together, we are being prepared or made ready for the next feast only God can can fulfill when the trumpet sounds and He takes us to our heavenly home.

These collectively-kept feast days are vital, but gathering together one or two days a year will not finish the work. They are intended to be springboards to fling us together into many collective forms of ministry for our community: compassionate outreaches to the poor and needy, sustained 24/7/365 prayer and praise before our God that He may bless the community, and unified evangelistic lifestyles[63] reaching out to everyone in the community. As the bride being made ready, we will accomplish this by walking in love, brimming with joy, and shining forth the resplendent beauty of His holiness! Altogether, this will be the worthy reception our King of kings greatly deserves! Let's keep the feasts of the Lord together until He comes for us! There is nothing more important. There is nothing more spectacular. Amen.

[62] www.gdopusa.com.

[63] www.LOVE2020.com